Warming Up the Chill

Teaching Against the Structures

Warming Up the Chill

Teaching Against the Structures

Laurie Milford
Jane Nelson
Audrey Kleinsasser

Editors

University of Wyoming

Warming Up the Chill
Teaching Against the Structures

Cover art: *Identity,* hand-colored intaglio by Sara Schleicher, a student of Mark Ritchie. The original of this piece is displayed in the ECTL, Coe Library, University of Wyoming, Room 307.

Book and cover design by Elizabeth Ono Rahel

ISBN 0-941570-25-8

Contents

Foreword

Barbara Azaria King, Chair, President's Advisory Council on Minorities' and Women's Affairs

In the fall of 2000, University of Wyoming President Philip Dubois created the President's Advisory Council on Minorities' and Women's Affairs (PACMWA), composed of faculty, students, staff, and administrators. The purpose of the council is to advise the president on issues that affect the recruitment and retention of minorities and women at the university, assess the institution's progress in diversity-related issues, and identify the most significant barriers to more successful recruitment and retention of minorities and women faculty and staff. The council has an annual pool of $75,000 to be used to promote diversity at the University of Wyoming. Operating within this charge, in the past two years we have played an instrumental role in heightening awareness about diversity issues on campus by posing questions and attempting to offer solutions.

In order to tie our questions and solutions to the campus community, we have invited campus constituents to propose projects or events that focus on diversity. Accordingly, the bulk of our annual $75,000 has been distributed to students, staff, and faculty in sponsoring a wide array of proposals, including outside speakers, several student retention projects, and the chilly classroom project that is the basis of this book. In all, the council has awarded nearly $140,000 through our competitive grants process. This sowing of seed money across campus has enhanced a multitude of efforts that seek to promote a greater understanding and appreciation of diverse life and work at a university.

The council sponsored the first competitive call for proposals in May of 2001. Especially important to the council has been a desire to fund diversity-related projects that show promise for on-going and wide campus appeal. One proposal that struck an immediate chord with the council was the Warming Up the Chill proposal authored by Audrey Kleinsasser and Jane Nelson, largely because the project applied directly to diversity issues across campus with broad implications for teaching and learning. Academic environments have often been characterized as chilly, and the University of Wyoming is not alone in facing challenges in creating and maintaining an environment that is warm, welcoming, and authentic. This project captures the essence of PACMWA's mission: to identify where the university falls short in creating and maintaining an environment that sincerely embraces individuals from all backgrounds and to propose strategies that improve diversity. Once the Ellbogen Center for Teaching and Learning received our funding, they were successful in securing regional and national awards. Specifically, the Ellbogen Center garnered $5,000 from the American Association for Higher Education and $3,000 from the Northern Rockies Consortium for Higher Education, essentially doubling their buying power while also gaining national and regional recognition of this unique and compelling project. The other really good news from this project has been the overwhelmingly positive response from students who eagerly nominated faculty who model the kind of environment that is far from chilly.

Warming Up the Chill continues to keep our attention. It has delivered everything contained in the original proposal and has grown beyond those initial boundaries into a far-flung yet focused analysis of what can occur when teachers and students work together. With this project documented in book form, a CD, and a website, all University of Wyoming faculty and students can easily access its findings, and other educational institutions can readily adopt its strategies. We congratulate the development, expansion, and completion of a project that provides a blueprint for faculty and students at UW and one that will continue to reap rewards for individual faculty and students, the university community, and other educational institutions. This has been one of the truly outstanding projects PACMWA has funded.

Acknowledgments

Staff members of the Ellbogen Center for Teaching and Learning have been unfailing in their support of this project. Robin Hill and her student staff in Instructional Computing Services have given essential technical support for the design and production of the project website and the CD-ROM. We want to especially thank Curt Brimhall and Jerry Blackburn. Andy Bryson and Shannon Powell in Instructional Media Services provided technical support for the videotaping of interviews and the inclusion of videotaped segments on the CD. Kimberly Coffrin, project coordinator at the ECTL, assisted in the grant-writing stages of this project. Danae Birch, senior office associate, has handled all emergencies and deadlines with grace, aplomb, and no small amount of skill.

Several colleagues at the University of Wyoming have helped to shape this project in important ways. Leellen Brigman, vice president for Student Affairs, alerted us to features of diversity that we had not considered. Dolores Cardona, assistant dean of Students for Multicultural Student Life, Judith Antell, director of American Indian Studies, Deborah McGriff, director of African American Studies, and Warnell Brooks, former student body president, provided important perspectives. Kathy Evertz, director of the University Studies First-Year Program, has helped us focus on the issues underscored in this project. As always, we acknowledge Rollin Abernethy in Academic Affairs for his continual support.

The President's Advisory Council on Minorities' and Women's Affairs (PACMWA), chaired by Barbara Azaria King, has been generous with funding for this project. The initiatives from this committee have made a difference at the University of Wyoming. The American Association for Higher Education (AAHE) provided us with a Going Public grant as a follow-up to UW's participation in their Campus Conversations initiative. We especially want to acknowledge Barbara Cambridge at AAHE. The Northern Rockies Consortium for Higher Education (NORCHE) provided additional funding to assist with this project.

Finally, we want to recognize Pat Hutchings and the Carnegie Foundation for the Advancement of Teaching for providing us with the models, philosophy, and encouragement necessary for undertaking this project.

Introduction: Taking Risks and Developing Leaders

Audrey Kleinsasser and Jane Nelson

As a collection, this set of cases profiles teachers who resolutely believe that students best learn the content of a course by engaging with each other and the teacher. To do that, students must step up and step out of past behaviors that are conventional and passive. Teachers must do the same. Unfortunately, institutional and instructional barriers prevent many students and teachers from making this kind of transformation. The chilly climates created by these barriers can be warmed by rethinking and rebuilding classroom structures.

Organized alphabetically, the set of cases illustrates a range of teaching assignments, undergraduate and graduate, in three of the seven University of Wyoming colleges. Donna Amstutz, adult education and technology, and Kent Becker, counselor education, teach graduate courses in the College of Education master's and doctoral programs. Dominic Martinez directs minority recruitment for the University of Wyoming and teaches in the University Studies first-year program. Mark Ritchie, from the art department, offers the perspective of someone who teaches in a studio setting and who advises many undergraduates seeking graduate school entrance. Julie Sellers teaches Spanish to sophomore and junior-level students who come to her classes with a wide range of language skills and experiences. Sally Steadman, from the College of Engineering, teaches freshmen and sophomores and advises several student groups, most of them focused on increasing the participation of women and minority students who are greatly underrepresented in the profession. These six teachers were selected from fifty-two University of Wyoming instructors who were nominated by students for their success in warming up chilly classrooms. The last chapter of this book contains a description of the nomination and selection process as well as an overview of the inquiry methods used to produce the case studies. In order to disseminate the information in this book as widely as possible, the project also features a CD-ROM and website. The CD can be found in the back pocket of this volume and includes video clips from the interviews as well as a resource section. To access the website, go to www.uwyo.edu/ctl.

The six cases illustrate how teachers and students take risks that challenge conventional teaching and learning structures. By taking risks, students also develop leadership qualities central to successful learning over a lifetime. While taking risks and developing leadership are common goals for students in undergraduate and graduate programs, these goals remain elusive for students hindered by chilly classroom climates. Put another way, within current structures, the students who most need to take risks and develop leadership skills are least likely to do so.

Bernice Sandler, senior scholar in residence for the National Association for Women in Education, coined the descriptor *chilly climate*. Sandler was interested in creating more positive learning climates for women. In this project, we have expanded Sandler's original concept to include students who are different or feel different by virtue of many factors, such as age, disability, ethnicity, gender, national origin, religion, sexual orientation, and socioeconomic background. These students frequently find that potential educational success is undermined by entrenched teaching practices and higher education's sometimes immutable structures. Teachers can help them to succeed by modifying instructional factors such as class organization, discussion strategies, office visits, assignments, lectures, and readings. We wanted to under-stand better and document such factors in a set of case studies that would feature teachers in different disciplines at different stages of their careers who teach both undergraduates and graduates.

Taking Risks: Teaching Against the Structure of Predictability and Safety

Most teachers want students to take intellectual risks that lead to deeper, richer learning and a more independent, self-determining life. Many students, however, appear to learn passively. They dutifully take notes in a lecture class and memorize the notes for an acceptable performance on a test, but they fail to make important connections that create a foundation for continued learning and for transfer to other classroom settings. Such students are anything but self-determining.

Teachers value independence for a variety of reasons. Many teachers are, themselves, self-determining learners. For them, the structure of academic disciplines makes sense. Because it makes sense, core principles of the disciplines might be less difficult to learn. Such teachers have made a career by focusing on disciplines that engage both mind and heart. They stay current with the literature as a matter of course. On their own, often with their own money, they join formal disciplinary organizations and regularly attend conferences. It's not surprising, then, that teachers value the independent learner who engages in class work by reading critically, asking good questions, and becoming involved in authentic work of the discipline. Teachers also value student self-determination because the burdens of teaching are lessened. Students know what to do, and do it well, with minimal prompting or coaching.

The students who nominated teachers for the Warming up the Chill project identified specific features of instruction that helped them learn what it meant to be more successful and self-determined. They recognized teachers who provided ample feedback and demystified academic procedures. Above all, the teachers were generous with their time, especially time during which their relationships with students built trust and confidence in learning. All of the teachers profiled in this book start small and in the same place to create trust. Each takes the time to learn names and establish relationships. Sometimes, the relationships extend beyond formal classroom boundaries. For students who may experience chilly classroom climates because of age, disability, ethnicity, gender, national origin, religion, sexual orientation, or socioeconomic background, a trusting relationship with the teacher emerges as central to developing confidence in learning. Perhaps more importantly, and central to the collaborations described below, students must know and be able to trust class colleagues. For this reason, the teachers profiled in this book expect students to work collaboratively with their fellow students.

From this clear-cut but necessary beginning, a classroom community takes shape. The teachers build a climate for learning and taking risks by creating opportunities for students to practice using their voices in ways that are new and demanding. Students communicate with the teacher and each other, and they participate in events outside of the classroom boundary.

In these six cases, getting personal goes beyond learning the names of students. For Dominic Martinez and Kent Becker, it often means getting to know students and their families in their home settings, and it means demanding that their students personally confront their fears or uncertainties about people with a different gender or sexuality or from a different race or class. For Mark Ritchie, it means establishing enough trust in a classroom so that his students can engage in the substantial critiquing process common in the visual and performing arts. Although Donna Amstutz, Sally Steadman, and Julie Sellers represent vastly different disciplines, they all illustrate in their chapters how conventional classroom assignments can create distance and anonymity, failing to establish personal and emotional connections for students. They believe that such assignments create barriers for student learning, and they offer persuasive arguments that emotional and personal connections lead to deep or internalized learning. Sally shows how standard engineering homework assignments or classroom exercises frequently contain gender bias. Donna and Julie show how textbooks can unrealistically depict entire categories of people or even exclude certain classes altogether.

Sally Steadman maintains that women learn differently from men and that minority group students learn differently from majority group students. All six authors in this book show how we all learn differently, affected by the variables of opportunity, motivation, time, and prior experience. The better teachers know students, the better teachers will be able to tailor reading selections and create assignments that are both worthwhile from disciplinary perspectives and engaging to students of varying ages and many backgrounds.

Learning to Be a Leader Through Collaboration: Teaching Against the Structure of Student Roles

Just as the six cases demonstrate how building relationships creates opportunities for risk-taking, they also show the value of collaboration in leadership development. The structure of schooling, especially in its grading systems and its emphasis on individual achievement, often becomes a barrier to one of the fundamental goals of a student: to grow into and think of oneself as a learner for life rather than as a good student in a one-semester course. How might students imagine being a civil engineer? A dual language teacher? A counselor? An artist for life? Just as important, what will it be like to work in an office or organization that values teamwork and collaboration? What kind of preparation in a classroom setting must students experience in order to become confident, self-determined learners? How might collaborations develop into leadership roles?

Again, the authors of these case studies start with small steps. Sally Steadman and Donna Amstutz convinced deans to replace individual desks with comfortable chairs and tables to facilitate collaborative learning. Dominic Martinez rearranges furniture and asks his students to find alternative spaces for class meetings. As these teachers build trusting relationships, they ask students to begin playing unfamiliar roles, such as teaching other students in problem-solving sessions, becoming elected class leaders responsible for evaluating the teacher, publicly critiquing each other's work, or assuming unusual speaking or acting roles. To assist students in these unaccustomed roles, the teachers become mediators and facilitators, often meeting one-on-one with students outside of class to provide additional support. One outcome of this leadership development is a distinct change in the classroom climate, where students talk with one another more as colleagues than as fellow students.

To supplement this classroom work, the case-study authors demonstrate a remarkable commitment to creating extracurricular leadership opportunities for their students. They travel with their students to conferences. They help to find funding for student research projects, international travel, and student productions. They help both individual students and groups to seize opportunities for leadership roles on campus. In these extracurricular roles, they model the collegiality and collaboration that they are asking their students to rehearse in the classroom.

The authors of these case studies confirm that the quality of the student-teacher relationship connects directly to the quality of the learning. An institution like UW offers numerous leadership opportunities for students, many of them separate from academic programs, such as student government, service organizations, religious institutions, and political parties. Students experiencing chilly classroom environments may be less likely to participate in co-curricular activities. Or, if they do, membership likely focuses around a restricted purpose that is far removed from their academic life. For all students, but especially those affected by chilly classroom climates, it's a distinct value to rehearse leadership in a classroom setting and be mentored by a teacher who connects academic, personal, and career goals.

Recommendations

Together, the six cases exemplify how instructional and curricular connections, created through relationships, warm up chilly classroom climates for students. The lesson of this project is clear: learning requires risk-taking. Students who already feel disadvantaged in a university setting because of age, disability, ethnicity, gender, national origin, religion, sexual orientation, or socioeconomic background are unlikely to take additional risks. These students need support to take necessary risks. Relationships are central to learning because students need the personal attention, which builds confidence and promotes leadership development.

Based on the case studies, we conclude with four specific recommendations that can be implemented by individual teachers. We also advocate discussion about the recommendations at program and curricular levels. If the teachers profiled in this book have made a positive difference in the lives of students, we can only imagine and celebrate the effects of department-wide initiatives.

1. Get personal, teacher to student; insist the same, student to student. Teachers in this collection make a commitment to learn student names and background information quickly. They know who's driving into campus for an evening class, who is sick, who might have demanding family obligations. They ask that students learn each other's names. These teachers are successful in persuading students that their interest is neither trivial nor infringing on privacy. Course syllabi and other classroom materials reinforce the difference getting personal makes.

2. **Take the risk of starting with what students know, including personal experiences. Create assignments that build on student knowledge and prior experiences.** The cases exemplify how the teachers build assignments that ask students to create connections between past learning and the content of the course. The assignments serve multiple purposes. They provide the teacher with information about students' knowledge, including writing abilities. The assignments reinforce the teacher's insistence that knowing names and something about each other is meaningful. Such assignments enable students to create personal connections with the content of the course. Finally, immediate feedback on these assignments enables students to make appropriate adjustments and practice self-determination.

3. **Create opportunities for in- and outside of class collaborations that show the real work of the disciplines, authentic engagement, and leadership development.** In this collection, the most powerful examples of learning come from assignments, projects, and events that provide students a glimpse into the discipline. Student engagement in learning increases by participating in conferences, critiquing one's own work and the work of others, and completing a project that has meaning outside of a classroom context. The teachers in this collection take considerable time, energy, and care in developing worthwhile, meaningful assignments that develop leadership.

4. **Be vigilant in book and instructional material selection.** For students susceptible to chilly classroom climates, instructional materials often distance, alienate, and discourage. All too frequently, the examples, charts, and graphics in textbooks unrealistically feature some classes of people and completely exclude others. If there's a way to choose a book that's more inclusive, do so. If not, create ways for students to critique the textbooks as they learn from them, or ask students to participate in efforts to find other materials.

Passion: For Teaching, For Learning, For Living

Donna Amstutz
Adult Learning and Technology

I am an associate professor and chair of the Department of Adult Learning and Technology. I have been at the University of Wyoming since 1991, except for two years when I taught for San Francisco State University. I teach courses in adult learning, educational issues of race, class, and gender, adult literacy, and community colleges. Like many faculty in my department, I have taught in distance formats for many

---

Dr. Amstutz incorporates a sensitivity to issues of race, class, and gender into all of her courses, and she models an excellent rapport with all students of various backgrounds. She does this by welcoming every student's viewpoints and comments without making a student feel as though her view lacks legitimacy. One really feels as though their background, no matter where they are coming from, is important to the conversation facilitated by this professor.

—Student nominator

years. I have developed two online courses that have been offered almost every semester, and I have also developed related websites for each class that provide graduate students with case studies and other forms of interactive learning. The College of Education granted me their teacher of the year award and also their award for the person who most contributed to the college climate. I have also received two university-wide advising awards. I live in Laramie with my husband, Tom, and I have one son, Justin, a daughter-in-law, Becky, and two grandchildren, Jordan and Mariah. To relax, I spend time with my dogs, Sam and Bambi. I enjoy painting and gardening, and I collect bird statues. I am committed to free expression, peace-making, and community activism.

I like to learn new things. It's one of my passions. Lifelong learning is something that needs to be modeled for students. In this project, I'm hoping to learn from other participants about new strategies for working with students as well as different issues I need to address. I am particularly interested in learning about specific strategies for teaching about socioeconomic class.

The Context of Work with Students

My area of expertise is race, class, and gender. In this area, I teach a class that's required of all graduate students in our department. We're talking about requiring it for all graduate students in the college, though I wouldn't necessarily teach it. It was about 1995 when I became concerned that there were few issues of diversity being covered in education unless a faculty member happened to have a particular interest in it. At that time, I developed the first course in race, class, and gender for the UW College of Education. Then I began to offer it statewide via compressed video. I would get teachers who were fascinated by this subject. I could tell there was a need in this state for conversations on these issues. So I've continued to teach it on compressed video and online, which is a real challenge. I've developed a CD that goes along with the class that we can send out to students. We have a website that has the whole course outlined. Since people learn differently, I think a variety of formats is helpful.

Education 3000, a required teacher education course, is an opportunity to ask students to think more broadly about teaching. When you're talking about diversity, in my mind, you have to attack it on many levels. Students here tend not to be receptive to issues of diversity because they think that's not what they are going to teach, particularly now that there is so much emphasis on standards, accountability, and teaching specific topics within each field. The state emphasizes standards; the national emphasis is on this too. The students are saying, "I don't need to learn about diversity. I'm going to teach in Buffalo, Wyoming. How much diversity is in Buffalo?" So we start there, talking about what kinds of diversity there are in Buffalo. They don't see, until you begin to open their eyes, the difference between the person who lives in a nice house and the person who lives in a trailer park. What are the stereotypes *they* have about those people? We continue asking such questions as, "Are you sure there are no Mexican Americans in Buffalo?" "Well, yeah, there are some who work in the fields," the students will say. All of a sudden it occurs to students that they live with diversity every day. I think it's helpful that I'm on oxygen and carry an oxygen tank, even when teaching. On the first day of class, I ask students to write down what they think

I'm going to be like as a teacher. They don't turn it in; they just keep it in their notebooks. Three weeks later, I ask them again what kind of teacher they think I am. Then I ask them to compare the two. It's amazing. They say after three weeks they don't even notice that I have oxygen. It's so much a part of me. The point to them is that when you see somebody who's different, you make a judgment. But you need to reserve the finality of that judgment for several weeks, or in some cases several months or several years, until you get a better indication of what that person is like.

It's important to reserve judgment on other issues as well, for example, issues of size. I talk about being fat. We talk about protecting fat kids in school, especially in the age of "everyone has to be thin." We know that in reality it's not true that everyone has to be thin, but we're still damaging kids. Even if all of these students can recall instances when they discriminated against other kids in school, they say, "I didn't know that was diversity."

I also teach The Adult Learner, which is a graduate course about how adults learn and about how the context of that learning is affected by race, class, and gender. We have about thirty-nine doctoral students and an equal number of master's students in our department, and many of them take courses only through distance mechanisms. They might be a teacher, a counselor, a vice president. Because community colleges serve primarily an adult population, the people who work in them look to us to get terminal degrees in adult education. We also have graduate students who are ministers and nurses and those who are training in business and industry—anyone who teaches adults. Much of the education in the military is adult education. We study how to develop curriculum in these settings.

In all of my classes, I teach about race, class, and gender. For example, when I teach The Community College, I offer alternative theories for contextualizing the role of the community college. Some people argue that community colleges are sorting systems, that we can't have everybody in the United States go to college and graduate. What would we do with them? In the view of many scholars, community colleges were developed to lower the expectations of people, primarily people of color. At least eighty percent of the people of color who go to college go to community college first. There, their aspirations are dumbed down. They might say, "I want to be a doctor." And the response is, "Why don't you be an x-ray technician or a nurse?" The belief is that community colleges have to fill the lower positions in society. Many people who work at community colleges never think of it that way. And of course this is just one interpretation of the role community colleges play. But it doesn't make any difference what course I'm teaching. I always try to broaden students' views of that course's content.

Teaching to the Whole Person
Inside the Classroom

It is my conviction that graduate school should not consist of a series of courses in which you get As or Bs and then a project (known as a dissertation) for which you research and write a long paper, and that's it for the doctoral program. That's not education. That's training or certification. To me, education involves the entire individual. It means that in class, you take care of students. Research is showing that learning is based on affective components of individuals. If students are frustrated, learning is not likely to occur. If they are in a comfortable environment, learning is more likely to occur. What do I mean by a comfortable environment? My class meets from 4:00 to 7:00. Often students haven't had a chance to eat because they're just getting off from work and coming to class. In every class session, I provide something to eat. It might be pretzels, fruit, candy, carrots and dip. It could be any number of things. Often students volunteer after the first couple of weeks to bring something.

Other aspects of the whole person include music. Often, when students are working on projects together, I'll play music—not just the music I like but music that they might like, music to expand their repertoire of listening, for example, Japanese music or Turkish dances. Most of the time, I use something that's relatively calm. Some people work better when they have this music surrounding them. You might think this doesn't make much sense. Well, there are a lot of things in the world that don't make much sense. But music might work for some people. It doesn't mean I do it everyday. There are some people who it frustrates.

Other ways of establishing a comfortable environment include attending to the physical need to move, which affects alertness. After the first hour, these adults in graduate classes perhaps begin to drift off. I don't do a lot of lecturing—I don't think that's the issue. But the students are relaxing from the day. So we'll get up and exercise. We'll do the bunny-hop around the room. You would think that adults would hate this, that they would consider this childish. But when you attend to the whole person, they love it. Later on in the semester, they'll tell me, "We need an exercise break. We need a wiggle break." (I call them wiggle breaks.) You know that sometimes kids just need to wiggle. Adults need to wiggle too, and after they do, they're ready to go on. They're ready to concentrate. This is teaching to the whole person. It's not just a set of tricky strategies. In my mind, food, music, and exercise reflect the idea that educating people means attending to who they are on an individual basis and providing for their needs.

Outside the Classroom

A couple of years ago, a few female doctoral students kept coming to me to talk. I asked them, "Why do you always come bother me? I'm not even your adviser." They said, "Because there are few professors who will talk about ideas with us as we develop our dissertations." I formed a group called the Goddesses. It's a group of female faculty and graduate students, and we meet once a month to study different goddesses, talk about how their symbolic meanings might relate to the process of writing a dissertation, or engage in relaxing activities. My husband calls this a séance, but the female faculty members say, "This is great. I can talk with other women without worrying about how I'm perceived by my male colleagues as an associate professor." It's a safe place. Once people graduate, they continue to come if they stay in Laramie. There's an ebb and flow. Some people might come twice and then decide they're too busy or that it's not for them. The group is by invitation only, not that I want to be exclusive but that we decided early on we wanted to be around people with whom we felt comfortable and safe. If we invited all female doctoral students and all female faculty, it would be a good activity, but it wouldn't be the same. So I try not to talk about it, and I ask the people who are involved not to talk about it because I don't want to hurt anyone's feelings. It's not that others are not good people but that this is a time when we—those who are involved—want to be comfortable. This is one way I teach to the whole person outside of class.

I also try to pay particular attention to foreign students. Sometimes the foreign students have difficulty when they arrive. Something may come up—a medical emergency or something similar. Perhaps they don't know where to go for help, or they can't afford to solve the problem. They would never, in my mind, ask to borrow money. I've never had that happen. As these students talk about the problems they have and I offer to lend them money, of course they tell me they're fine, that they don't need money. If they don't have groceries and they won't take money, I'll go buy groceries and take them to their house. If it's about a car, I'll say, "Take it over to this shop; I'll talk to the owner and ask if you can make payments." If the shop doesn't allow payments, I'll pay the bill, and the student can pay me. Certainly, many people are not going to ask for this kind of help. But we're talking about teaching to the whole person. How can an international student concentrate if he or she can't feed his or her family because he or she doesn't have enough money due to some other emergency?

I might say to an international student, "You've been down for a couple of days." It's an observation. They could be down for any number of reasons. He or she will say, "Oh no, I'm fine." I might then ask, "How's your family?" The student will tell me his or her family is fine. I'll push, saying, "Well there is something that's bothering you." The student might then admit that he or she has been having difficulties at home but will usually insist that the problem is taken care of. I'll ask whether there's any way I can help. "Oh no, I'm taking care of it." "Do you have electricity? Do you have gas to cook on? Is it anything like that? I just want to make sure you're safe." It takes a long time to drag out the reasons. It's not being nosey—it's being persistent—so that the student's needs are taken care of. "Well, we've just spent our last ten dollars, and we don't have any milk for the baby." At this point, I offer to buy the milk. "No, no, we will find a way. I would never take any money from you." I may say, "Come with me; I need to run an errand." So I take the student to the grocery store, and we pick up some milk. I will then walk over to the vegetables and to the fish counter and buy some of these items for myself, casually picking up enough for the student's family as well. We get to the checkout, and I pay for all of the groceries. Then I drop the student off at his or her house and say, "These groceries are yours." The student knows that food worries for that week are over. The student also knows that he or she can come to me. I may not have everything this student needs, but I will do what I can to help.

I find a lot of students, especially American students, might have problems with a divorce, their child, a job. They'll come to see me and say, "I'm really having a hard time right now." What I think they want is someone to listen. The problem for professors is that if you do this with all of your students, you would have no time. You have to find a balance. Also, not everyone helps students in the same way. In other words, there are many professors who would not buy food for a student but who would spend an extra two hours explaining a difficult concept to a student. That's as valid as buying food. We all have different things to offer. In the *me, me, me* environment, some faculty say, "I don't have time," or "I can't be here after 5:00." You do have to set limits, but your job isn't just teaching for three hours, two days a week. Your job, as an educator,

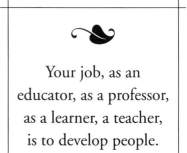

Your job, as an educator, as a professor, as a learner, a teacher, is to develop people.

as a professor, as a learner, a teacher, is to develop people. A professor might say, "I'm here to teach my field, not to develop people." I'll respond, "What's your definition of a professional in that field? Is communication important? Is caring about others important?" You're dealing with the whole person.

Different students need different things. It might not be food; it might not be extra help with a difficult assignment. It might be that you need to tell a student that other students perceive her to be arrogant. She will say, "Oh, I don't intend to be arrogant!" I'll tell her, "Well, I don't think you ever intend to be that way. You're very reserved; it's difficult for you to share your opinions. Other students perceive that to be arrogant." The student tells me she doesn't want to be perceived that way and asks what she can do. I'll suggest that we practice holding a conversation in which she shares her thoughts. Some instructors might work well with students on communication; others might give extra time.

Fostering All Voices

Psychological comfort in the classroom is also important. I want people to feel they can ask any question they need to ask. It's crucial to set a comfortable environment. I let students know that their opinions, although they may differ from mine, are valid opinions. For example, in Wyoming, I've found a lot of resistance to teaching about homosexuality, even mentioning it. But in a course on race, class, and gender, you have to deal with issues of sexual orientation. Then I came to find out that many people are strongly opposed to any mention of homosexuality in schools because of their religious beliefs. Of course this is true in other places too, but here I found it more pronounced.

So the students and I start talking about homosexuality, and without telling them my opinion, I let the students debate the issues. Usually their rationales are based on philosophical or religious grounds. So we talk about how you can attack someone's faulty logic and how you can attack poor or incorrect information. But it's not helpful to attack someone's belief system. There you have to take a longer-term approach. I affirm students who vehemently oppose homosexuality. I say, "Jerry, you represent the opinions of many people in the United States. What we're hoping to do is get more dialogue between people who have different views."

Students may ask me what my views are. We hear this myth that teachers have to be neutral. That's B.S. I think we've raised children— now adults, who are in graduate or undergraduate classes—who don't think very much. They're trained not to think. They're trained to give the right answer or to complete multiple-choice tests. But they're not trained to think, to form an opinion. One of the reasons this happens is that their teachers say, "Well, I don't want to give you my opinion. It wouldn't be appropriate." So nobody knows what teachers think and why. I also believe this "neutralism" is based on the idea that many people want to avoid argument or conflict at any cost.

When we have a discussion, about homosexuality for example, and students ask me for my opinion, I will say, "The issue, in my mind, is not so much about sex as it is about affiliation. Every time we talk about heterosexuals, do we talk about their sex lives? No. So why should we, when we're talking about homosexuals, think about them only in terms of their sex lives? Ninety percent of the time, they're cooking, they're driving through the car wash, they're doing all of these other things that heterosexuals do. We take one little piece of the homosexual life and say it's wrong. You can have a religious belief, and that's your opinion. You're entitled to that. But on the other hand, other people are entitled to their opinions as well." All of a sudden, my graduate students who are vehemently opposed to homosexuality will say, "I hadn't thought about it like that. It is just a small part." One of my students told me, "I still don't believe that homosexuality is right, but now I'm more comfortable around homosexuals because I see what you're saying—that sex is just a very small part of the life style." Maybe ten years from now that person will have developed some more and will look back and say, "Yeah, Donna said something about that kind of thing." Not that I want them to remember me, but I want them to see the cumulative experience of education. That's one example of how you set a comfortable environment—you need to validate your students even though you may not agree with their opinions.

I don't give students my opinion until after I'm sure they have voiced their opinions and after I'm sure that they feel safe in the classroom. However, I believe that I should give them my opinion after theirs, particularly the reasons for my beliefs. Then I emphasize that my opinion is not the only one. It was formed on my past experiences and my family—beliefs that were passed on to me and my own analysis of situations. Since everyone has different past experiences, I recommend tolerance of other's beliefs. This is particularly true of some "liberal" students who think that people who don't agree with their notions about a subject are uninformed or mean spirited. I continually struggle with helping students see that our value systems are based on what we were taught, our social group, and the environment in which we were raised. I try to get them to see that if, perhaps, they had been raised similarly to the people whose opinions they don't like, they might hold those exact opinions. Teaching tolerance goes in both directions. You must support learners as they struggle with their conflicts while encouraging them to reflect on the assumptions they've based their beliefs on.

Once you give students permission, once they're comfortable saying what they think, some students still find it difficult to voice a point of view. A lot of students tell me they've never before been asked what they think. It's hard for them. Some students would rather have you tell them *x, y,* and *z.* They can memorize it and get on with their lives. That's not graduate education.

Warming up the chill, that is, providing a safe environment, means that professors occasionally take themselves out of the center, step to the margins, look at everyone in the classroom as co-learners, and put students in the center. This gives them the chance to ask what a given student really needs. There will be students whose needs you can't meet; there will be those who are doing fine, who don't need anything from you. It's intuitive. A lot of professionals, especially professors, downplay intuition. But the more I've studied, the more I find out about how women see things more holistically than men. Just recently a former student sent me a study that argues that women use a much broader area of their brains to make sense of the world than men. Men use primarily the left half. Women and men do think differently; they *know* differently. I'm not saying that all women know intuitively, and I'm not saying that all men don't know intuitively. I know men and women who are exceptions to this pattern. But we have to make generalizations in order to make sense of the world—that's one of the things you want to convey when you're talking about diversity. To take gender differences—using intuition, for example—men *tend* to cluster at one end of the spectrum; women *tend* to cluster at the other end. There's nothing wrong with either tendency, and some men are included with the "female" view and some women relate to the "male" view.

Warming up the chill, that is, providing a safe environment, means that professors occasionally take themselves out of the center, step to the margins, look at everyone in the classroom as co-learners, and put students in the center. This gives them the chance to ask what a given student really needs.

When I use intuition, it's not that I say, "What can I intuit today?" It just happens. I'll come back to my office after class and think, "That didn't go very well." All of a sudden, it will hit me: "Jeremy—there's something going on with Jeremy." It's not necessarily negative—it might be that Jeremy is doing much better than he was at the beginning of the semester. These things just click. Sometimes you ask students about it, you comment on it; sometimes you don't. Sometimes you know that students don't want you to comment. You have to walk a fine line between pressing and not pressing. Many instructors will say, "It's not my job to ask students about their personal lives." I say we can't make a lot of progress without gently pushing people. You never know if you can fly unless someone pushes you off the cliff. Understand, as an educator, I'm not going to take you to a high cliff; I'm going to take you to a low one, so if you fall, you're not going to be hurt—your self-esteem won't disappear forever.

With regard to fostering women's voices, I still do not allow my students to say "you guys." They say it doesn't mean anything. I ask them what *guy* means and whether that refers to a man. They respond, "Yeah, okay, but it's not important." I encourage them to think about it, suggesting, "Every time you say, 'you guys' why don't you say 'you girls' or 'you gals?'" I ask the men, "How would you like that? What do you think 'you guys' does to women?" It's subconscious. I talk about how even though this is an important issue for me, every so often I catch myself saying "you guys." It's difficult to change our behavior. I don't want people to be politically correct all the time. I just want people to do their best so that other people feel included—or at least not excluded for reasons we can control.

In Wyoming, I talk a lot about diversity in terms of religion: Latter Day Saints, Catholicism, Methodism, Judaism, Muslims. Students will comment that they find one religious practice or another really weird. I'll ask them what religion they are and then point out that other people of other religions may find their practices and traditions strange. You try to shine a light on their assumptions. Many people have not examined their assumptions. It's these assumptions that get them into trouble.

Some will say, "I don't know why race is a big deal. Everybody has an equal opportunity." I hear it all the time in my classes when we start talking about race. I'll say, "You know, on Thursday, I'm going to bring pictures of the school my son went to in Chicago." It has a six-foot fence around it with barbed wire on the top. It has bars on the windows and a locked front door. This is an elementary school. The school includes children who live in a homeless shelter right across the street. These children might be at this school for forty days and then be gone. This school has kids who eat only in the morning, in the breakfast program, and at lunch—at school. We talk about funding. Because schools are often based on local wealth, a school in a prosperous urban suburb might spend $8,000 per year on a student. A school in an inner-city district, where there is no industry, little tax base, and only run-down housing, might spend $5,000. Is that equal opportunity? We should talk not about equal opportunity but about equal outcome. What is it that we can do that will give equal outcome? So we talk about money, how it's distributed, and who gets money for what reasons. Are people poor because they want to be poor? It's amazing to me how many of my students say yes. To me, that's blaming the victim. Ninety-nine percent of people who are poor were born poor.

We talk about other examples as well. Two people graduate from college—one from a middle-class family and one from a very poor family. They both graduate from college, they both get married, and they both have two kids. They want to buy a house. The person from the middle-class family gets a loan because her parents can cosign. The other person's mother is on welfare. *She* can't sign a loan. So even at this point, life's opportunities are different.

Race, class, and gender are things that people have beliefs about. You can't counter beliefs with logic; you can only counter them with facts. But your beliefs affect the way you interpret facts. You can't rely only on facts. You ask, "How do I get these people to think differently? How do I get them to feel differently?" You can say, "The theory of multicultural education is x, y, and z." Students aren't going to internalize it. You say, "What are you going to do when you have two kindergartners and one says to the other, 'My daddy says I can't play with you anymore because you don't believe in Jesus. You're Jewish.' What do you do as a teacher?" The students can start thinking about it. I use lots of case studies and role playing, asking the students to take on the position of responsibility. If they then say, "It's not the teacher's role to do anything," I'll push them further: "That's a position you can take. But do you understand that that reinforces the status quo? It tells the one girl that it's okay to say hurtful things. It tells the other girl that no one will protect her or stick up for her." These are things students haven't thought about. They think they'll be neutral and that that will be okay. But neutrality reinforces the status quo.

It amazes me that at the graduate level, many students from Wyoming haven't considered these things. Some have. By and large, I see many people here—I think because it's rural with a low population—who haven't thought about these issues.

I write about body size. We used to have desk chairs in the Education Building—the chairs with the small desk attached. I couldn't fit in them. I told the dean that these were not appropriate seats for adult learners. He'd never thought about it before. He couldn't change the equipment immediately, but he could place in every room a few chairs without arms. If people are of large size, they would have a place to sit without being embarrassed. That's activism. That's a passion for giving all students a voice.

I joined the National Association to Advance Fat Acceptance (NAAFA), and I've given presentations and written papers at the national level on issues of body size in education. Teachers reinforce the stereotypical body image by discriminating against fat children. They tend not to like fat children because fat is something they fear. This plays out in recess, for example, where teachers tend to talk with thin children but not with fat children. They will often make comments about a kid's size. This is just as bad as commenting on a child's color. When they're monitoring lunch, they'll say to a fat child, "You know you're not supposed to eat dessert." These remarks tell a child that he or she is not good enough, that he or she is different and needs to look thin, like most of the other children. So the national association has come up with some guidelines for teachers. For example, do not use stories where fat characters are portrayed negatively, as a slob or as stupid, for example. Lobby textbook publishers to include larger children. One study compared the Dick and Jane books of the 1920s to books used in second through fourth grades now. Over that time period, books have come to represent girls as twenty-five percent smaller. The boys didn't change. This was probably done unintentionally, but it reflects society's preoccupation with body size. It's important to educate future teachers about this form of discrimination because it's a struggle to get people to accept these differences. There is so much hurt. Fat teenagers are committing suicide because they can't take the teasing any longer. We need to educate teachers to protect these children just as they defend children of color or gay teenagers. Let's protect fat kids. They are just as powerless in changing their size as people of color are in changing their color or homosexuals are in changing their sexual orientation. Few people realize that. It's my passion to get people to understand so that people who come behind me—my son's children—will have a better, more accepting world. My son is about 300 pounds. Most likely, his children are going to be fat. If we can look past this, we see intelligence, wisdom, and kindness. We must not be blinded by difference—that is the goal.

A past vocational education student decided to look at the textbooks in his field. He began this study insisting that there were no issues of race, class, or gender in vocational education. But he found that ninety percent of the textbook illustrations used men. Every pronoun is "he" or "him." He realized that a third of his students in vocational education are girls. Yet girls represent only ten percent of the illustrated students in the textbooks he was using. This student will still call me—ten years later—to say he's found another example. Once your eyes are opened, you see everything differently. My passion is transmitted in the student who, as the semester unfolds, will look at textbooks and ask whether fat children and girls are represented or identify other diversity issues that previously they would not have been aware of.

The Teacher-Student Relationship: Negotiating Power

I tell students in the first class and again in the second class, "If you have any questions, feel free to come to my office. If you can't make my office hours, just give me a call. Or better yet, email me; I respond quickly to email. I'll be happy to set up a time." A lot of professors can say that, but students won't believe it because in the classroom, the students are not comfortable. Once the professor establishes comfort, establishes a group of co-learners, including the professor, then the students will come to the office. They will come when you don't want them to!

Teachers who look different, who don't meet the American ideals for physical appearance, often face disrespect in the classroom. Many students will not respect you as much as they would if you met their expectations of what they think professors *should* look like. Professors who are people of color tell me students challenge them when they don't believe those same students would challenge a professor who is white and male.

As a person of size I encounter something similar. When I weighed almost 450 pounds, other faculty members looked at me as though I weren't smart enough to be a professor. They seemed to suggest that if I was stupid enough to let myself get into that position, then I was too stupid to be a professor. Well, I didn't have control over my size. That's the myth—that fat people have control over their weight. Why would you want to be something that is so painful and hurtful? I find particularly obnoxious people who exercise a lot who assume that fat people don't exercise, that they are unhealthy. Many fat people are healthy. They don't have high blood pressure, for example. At 450 pounds, I was swimming several times a week. I was exercising, doing laps and water aerobics on a regular basis. One study of fasting at the National Institute of Health found that even after six weeks with no food—nothing—some participants actually gained weight. We have studies showing that thin people eat as much if not more than fat people. It comes down to differences in metabolism and chemical makeup and genes. People process food differently. How do I educate people who are otherwise well-meaning that all fat people are not unhealthy? They live great lives and are consumed with passions that don't have anything to do with weight. It's the same with homosexuality and issues of color. Differences must be appreciated. A lot of people discriminate against others because they have not educated themselves about these issues. They assume that what they know is always correct and complete.

Role Models

As students graduate and become faculty members themselves, I try to model for them that they need to take care of their students. I'm a Mennonite. I grew up without radios and wearing bonnets—there were all of these things you could and couldn't do. It was important in this religion that you don't tell people what to do; you simply take care of their needs. I don't tell future teachers they need to take care of their students. But as I take care of their needs, they may ask, "Why are you helping me?" At that point, I will explain that it's part of my ethic. The college I went to, Goshen College, requires every student to go abroad for fourteen weeks, seven of which are spent studying geography, language, and social-economic issues. The other seven weeks are spent doing service. Goshen students continue to receive invitations to return to the places they go because they don't proselytize; they simply ask, "What do you need? How can I help you fix your window?" They don't ask or say anything about how the window might have been broken. They just fix it.

Who we are depends on where we were born, who raised us, the environments we have been involved in. If you like classical music, in most cases you grew up listening to classical music. If you like R&B, most likely you grew up listening to it. If your mother or father—most likely your father—is a coal miner, chances are you will grow up to be a miner or work in a related field. Why do we struggle so hard against this? Why don't we simply say, "This is what I believe; this is who I am." If people ask, I might talk about my Mennonite background and how I came to this way of teaching to the whole person. You just do it. You have to do it. If you don't, it wouldn't feel right.

When I explain this ethic to others, they can begin to see that people they have difficulties with may be difficult because their experiences led them there. It doesn't mean they're going to like everyone they come across. But they have a better understanding that people who hold different values came to them through the experiences they have had. If a woman had affirming and supportive parents or caretakers and a generally positive upbringing, as an adult she will have different beliefs than someone who had a single mother who was addicted to crack. Not that someone who is a single parent and addicted to drugs would be a negative caregiver—that's not a very good example. I've just used a stereotype. I have to guard against that myself. But sometimes it's good for students to see that it happens.

Passion is what drives most people who work to foster equality. They experienced something in their past—either negative or positive—that made them begin to think about gender or other differences, usually a specific type of difference. Perhaps they had been discriminated against because of their gender. In my case, it was much more. When I was young, my sister married an African man in 1963. They were both going to the University of Chicago. My parents said that was fine, they didn't have any problems with the marriage, but they were concerned that if my sister and her husband had children, they would face challenges because of the mixed-race marriage. So this dialogue had been going on in my family for some time. When I went to college, because I was fat I didn't fit in the social arena. There was a group of us who started hanging out together. Some were African American, some were gay, one was an international student, one woman was very tall; I was the only fat person. We bonded because all of us, in our own way, stood outside the normative community. Soon, one of these friends invited me into African American culture, where I discovered that African American culture does not emphasize body size. As he explained to me, African American females are never going to achieve the "American" (meaning white) ideal of blond, blue-eyed, willowy women. It's impossible. Therefore, they look at people more realistically. If you're large, you're large. In the white community, you simply are not accepted. At that college age, which is a crucial age for many people, I was accepted into my black friend's family. They would ask me to visit even when my friend wasn't able to be there. Suddenly, a whole new world opened to me. I felt appreciated and loved.

Once you have dealt with one kind of prejudice, then you begin to recognize it in other places. Something clicks and you suddenly

American culture tries to move toward one idealized, unrealistic expectation. But I say there is a full range of human beings—their conceptions of beauty, their sexual orientations cover a spectrum. You don't have to like what I wear, you don't have to like the way I look, but you do need to respect that these are my choices. Likewise, I'm going to respect your choices.

understand discrimination. The passion of trying to get people who have not really thought about these things before furthers one's efforts in the world. The passion I have is demonstrated in my office. On my door, you'll see a poster showing fat women that says, "Beauty comes in all sizes." You'll see on my wall a poster showing a plaster cast of a real body, the real bodies that people have. The majority of American women wear size fourteen or above—the majority. American culture tries to move toward one idealized, unrealistic expectation. But I say there is a full range of human beings—their conceptions of beauty, their sexual orientations cover a spectrum. You don't have to like what I wear, you don't have to like the way I look, but you do need to respect that these are my choices. Likewise, I'm going to respect your choices.

Part of the problem with a lot of liberals on campus is that they become antagonistic toward people who don't hold the same view, who are not as liberal, for example. To me they are doing the same thing that they criticize society for doing to the ideals liberals champion. I want to make it clear—I do think people have to stand up for the things they believe in. One has to stand up and say what's right and wrong, for example, in the case of Matthew Shepard's murder. But you never attack the people who disagree, even if they attack you. That rule comes from my Mennonite background, and Mennonites teach nonviolence. We don't serve in the military, we do alternative service. We always try to turn the other cheek.

When I'm harassed on the street because I'm fat, those assaults are difficult to deal with. Some people in the fat-acceptance movement argue that you should be rude back. But I think it's better to counter with kindness. When you're walking around in a large crowd, at a fair for instance, and a child points at you and says, "Look at the fat woman!" it's good to say, "And aren't I beautiful? Isn't it beautiful that I'm fat and you're skinny and your daddy's tall, and your sister's short? Isn't is beautiful that we're all different?" You're educating the child but also the parent. Being fat is not something to be embarrassed about; it's a descriptive word, just like short or tall, blond or brunette.

We have to be aware that every day, in every circumstance, we're modeling something for the world. I have a poster on the wall of my office of Langston Hughes. When African American students come in, maybe they will see that a black American is represented as a scholar and leader. I have a button that says, "Straight but Not Narrow." I have a pink triangle. People who have a different sexual orientation than mine can come into my office and know that this is a safe place for them. I have a poster representing labor. I remember working at a very low wage for a long time, and I have a lot of friends who are working-class. People who have a working-class background can come in and know they can talk about that. They don't need to worry that I will judge them. That's modeling. That's showing my passion. I cannot live in the world without trying to make it better.

Antonio Gramsci says that many people are intellectual. Some people are educated intellectuals; some people are uneducated or organic intellectuals. It's like wisdom. Wisdom means experience and values and knowledge about a lot of things. It's not education that gives you wisdom. Wisdom comes from experience. And, to be wise, one must accept people for who they are. They should respect all views—not necessarily accept them—but surely respect a person as a valuable human being, regardless of belief or value system.

Epilogue

Whatever you do in your classroom—syllabi, texts, other course materials—reflects the America that you want America to be. If students are white supremacist (and I've had a few who have told me they are), then I say to them, "When you imagine your ideal world, you're going to imagine white people in it. That does not bother me as long as you take no action against people who have a different vision." This is America: you can have any thought you want as long as you don't act on it in a negative way.

My girlfriend's son, Jamil, is very dark. Her son and my son grew up together. When they were small, in elementary school, Jamil complained that one of the other kids in school kept calling him "nigger." Vanessa, my friend, talked to the teacher. The name-calling continued. So Vanessa talked with the principal. The principal said, "We've got to deal with this," and he called in the parents. He told the parents it seemed their son was calling another child "nigger." The parents responded, "What's wrong with that? That's what we call them at home." And the principal then told the parents—educators have to understand they can do this—

"When you are in your own home, you're free to say whatever you want. But when your child comes to school, there are certain rules. One of the rules is that children cannot devalue others by using certain language." I try to make it clear that this is what educators have to do.

My son, here in Laramie, has been told to go back to Africa. He too has been called a nigger. This was twelve years ago. At first I assumed it was the lower-class rednecks, the cowboys. But as it turned out, the children who were calling my son "nigger" were children of professors. So I asked myself, "What makes you think that professors would not have as broad a range of opinions as you find among other groups with other levels of education?" You learn not to make assumptions about anything.

The notion that we are all going to move forward at the same pace at every place in the United States is an impossible dream. There is nothing wrong with having a dream, a vision. If you humiliate other people, you will never build bridges. There are issues for which you should not lash back. You don't want to do the same thing that the person you disagree with is doing to you. You have to honor and respect people, no matter what they believe. I got the idea of honoring from a past Native American student who taught me to honor all things, that honoring the earth includes honoring all people. I don't have to like you outside of class. I don't have to hang around you outside of class. But when you're in my class, you have to feel that your opinion is as protected as anybody else's. That's not just in the discipline of education—or in courses on race, class, and gender. That's true in every class, whether it's art or physics. Someone in one of the science departments told me, "There's no discrimination in science." To that I say, "Get real." If there's no discrimination in science, why do you have such a tiny minority of ethnic-minority students in the sciences? It's not intentional, but it's there. It's institutional. Look at your content area broadly and ask how you might be—unknowingly—excluding people who are not like yourself. In summary, affirm people's inherent worth. Agitate. Educate. Honor everything. Honor everyone.

Spirituality in Teaching: Connecting with the Person First

Kent Becker

Counselor Education and Supervision

As a counselor educator, my primary responsibility is to assist in the preparation of master's and doctoral level counselors and educators in the areas of community counseling, school counseling, and student affairs practice. I currently serve as the program coordinator for our doctoral program in counselor education and supervision, co-coordinator of our marriage and family therapy specialization, and clinic director. My professional passion and clinical emphasis is marriage and family therapy. I

Dr. Becker can make even the driest material interesting and welcoming. He uses many creative strategies to capture interest and encourage participation. He is careful to introduce diversity issues, and he established a diversity training program on campus. You cannot help but be comfortable and feel a sense of community in his classes.

—Student nominator

---

maintain professional licensure as both a marriage and family therapist and as a professional counselor.

I graduated in the fall of 1994 with a doctorate in counselor education and supervision. Throughout my doctoral work I served as an instructor at a local community college teaching a variety of psychology courses. After completing my EdD, I worked as a family therapist and supervisor. Prior to coming to UW, I taught fulltime at a small state college in Nebraska. I taught fifty percent graduate and fifty percent undergraduate courses. At UW my classes are, for the most part, all graduate-level, master's and doctoral. My courses are a mix of theory and practical application, helping counselors-in-training make the leap from concepts to practice. The large majority of our students are working toward licensure—either as a licensed professional counselor, licensed addictions therapist, or licensed marriage and family therapist.

The timing for participating in this project is interesting. As I enter into my tenure year, I find myself less and less focused on the very thing that I love to do the most, teaching. Instead, my energies have increasingly been consumed by meetings, committees, writing, becoming a "leader in my field," and so on. It is time for me to slow down and reflect upon my teaching—on what works and what doesn't. While I talk with doctoral students about teaching, we rarely focus on *my* teaching—we focus on their teaching. For selfish reasons, I am also hoping to connect with others who similarly view teaching as a passion. Timing is funny. I seem to be involved in this project so that I can remember why I am in the academy—to teach.

The Context of Work with Students

People often ask what draws a person to the field of psychotherapy. Is it an indirect means to heal thyself? Or is it a calling to make a difference? For me, it is a balance between both. Being an educator and a counselor provides me with a structure to connect with what is important and critical in the human condition—the heart and soul. This field has also allowed me to reflect, self-confront, and stretch myself personally. I believe that I am a better person, man, husband, and father because I am constantly surrounded by and engaged in conversations of family, love, partnership, and commitment.

Family is central to both my professional and personal orientation. Family is everything—both in pain and healing. Understanding my clients, students, loved ones, and self from a systemic perspective provides me with a foundation that, I believe, is compassionate, strength-based, and hopeful. Whether I am at home with my family, in the classroom, in session with a couple, or in a meeting on campus, the basic constructs of my field are always present and in motion—systems at work.

Several of the classes I teach are focused on marriage and family therapy. At least half of my courses are clinical practicums during which students are providing supervised counseling to clients in our clinic here on campus. My department runs a free clinic for children, adolescents, families, and adults that complements the University Counseling Center and the Department of Psychology's training clinic. One evening a week my colleague David Carson and I supervise a marriage and family clinic/practicum in which our students work with several couples and families. Every session is videotaped and we observe sessions live through a one-way mirror or an observation monitor. Teaching students to work with couples and families is the highlight of my week. Students grow and face their own insecurities at a rate that is exhilarating. It is an honor to see clinicians grow in competence and confidence while they are providing a quality product to the university and larger community. I leave each clinic evening exhausted and wired—knowing that something good and meaningful is happening.

Teaching to the Whole Person

We talk about holistic approaches a lot in the field of counseling and therapy. My primary theoretical foundation is in family systems. That means when I'm helping a student work with a client, we try to understand the client—whether this is an individual, couple, or family—from a broader systems view. We are understanding them in terms of what's going on with them—in their family, their family of origin, their cultural and spiritual context, their environmental context—and what's going on for them historically. We look at the whole person to try to understand them. A client might come in at 10:00 a.m. with a specific presenting concern, such as depression, anxiety, or a marital problem, and another client at 11:00 a.m. with the identical presenting concern. Both clients may be struggling with depression, let's say, but the context of their lives—physical and spiritual—makes all the difference in the world. It's the same with teaching. I try to take the same approach with students.

Spirituality—in the broadest sense of the word—is an area of increasing professional interest and research in counseling and counselor education. How do we, as counselors and counselor educators, better incorporate people's spiritual beings and their spiritual lives into the counseling and healing process? In the past, as counselors, a lot of us have thought we weren't supposed to intrude on an individual's spirituality. Now, as I've gotten a little older, I realize that you just can't separate the spiritual from the mental and physical. I also do not define spirituality as narrowly as I used to. I see spirituality as the daily ways in which we connect with each other, our faith, nature, and so on. When things come together in the classroom or with a student, it tends to be when the spiritual issues come up—between people in the class or between myself and the students or clients I'm working with.

We often talk about parallel process in my field. Parallel process, in training, exists when an issue or dynamic occurring in session is mirrored in supervision or the educational process. For example, power dynamics in session between partners may be mirrored in the co-therapy relationship and/or between the therapist and supervisor. For me, it provides an opportunity to explore the connection between the two systems—a physical manifestation of the spirit at work.

My field allows me more latitude getting to know students than other fields might. When people come through the door, we make it clear, particularly at the master's level, that fifty percent of their work will be academic and fifty percent will be personal. This does not mean that they're coming in for personal counseling but that we expect them to walk as many paths as possible before they ever have the right to ask somebody else to walk a similar path. We expect people to share their hearts and souls more than most programs might. We expect it in the context that that's what it takes to be a fully functioning human being and an effective counselor. If I'm sitting here with a client, asking that person to work on something, I have to be doing my own personal work as well.

In the introductory family therapy course, students are expected to do their own family-of-origin work. They have to look at their own families, develop an extensive genogram (which is similar to a family tree), and analyze how patterns within their family impact their current functioning and their future role as a counselor. I always try to make that link. Any time I give an assignment with a personal component, it has to be very clear that the link is to the students' work as counselors. I'm not being voyeuristic.

The "self" piece is very purposeful in the courses of our programs, not just mine, but in most of the classes in the department. Assignments are designed to encourage self-reflection and opportunities for students to openly and honestly challenge themselves. At times these dialogues evolve into small group discussions (if appropriate) and/or impromptu visits after class. I continue to be impressed with our students' willingness to take these personal risks—just the thing that good counselors are made of.

Then, too, some students will approach me, or I'll approach them, when they are having trouble with the academic portion of the program. This doesn't happen often—we screen pretty heavily, and candidates for admission have to demonstrate a strong academic record. In these rare cases, I try to be as direct and understanding as possible. These students are typically struggling on an interpersonal level, and their struggle is getting in the way of their professional potential. The direction of these conversations is as varied as the student—I tend to take each one on an individual basis.

Counseling practicum and the dissertation phase of the doctoral program tend to be the times when my relationships with students are the most critical. Practicum typically involves six to ten students. This is a semester-long experience during which students are seeing clients in our clinic. Practicum is the time when students are the most excited, anxious, and vulnerable as they are actively striving to become counselors. It is a time when individual and group dynamics are the loudest as students are inundated with new experiences and a variety of feedback from both faculty and peers. During most semesters, I am both a practicum instructor and an individual supervisor to a handful of students. This means that I have several opportunities each week to support students in their continued professional development.

As a designated supervisor, I meet with students weekly. While the majority of the time is focused on their cases and/or their professional development, it is common for students to reach a time when they're struggling with something that's getting in the way of their counseling. At these times I work with their struggles only to the point where we identify and clarify what might be going on. I help them to figure out what they're going to do next. My role is not to be their counselor but to help them identify the issues. It's hard to show people parts of themselves that they don't particularly want to look at. This work is difficult, but it's also a wonderful part of what I do. When students share their personal lives, I consider it a compliment. If students do need to do their own personal work, they are encouraged to do so outside the department— to further respect their privacy.

My role is not to be their counselor but to help them identify the issues. It's hard to show people parts of themselves that they don't particularly want to look at. This work is difficult, but it's also a wonderful part of what I do. When students share their personal lives, I consider it a compliment.

The Student-Teacher Relationship: Negotiating Power

Inside the Classroom

My students call me Kent. At the beginning of a course, I say, "My name is Kent Becker. My preference would be that you call me Kent. If you want to call me something different, I'd prefer Dr. Becker rather than Mr. Becker," and then I often joke, "because I'm still paying for my degree." It takes some of them a little while to get used to this—but not very long. I did this even in Nebraska, where I taught many more undergraduates. For some international students, it's more culturally appropriate for them to stay with Dr. Becker, and I'm comfortable with that as well.

For whatever reasons, I use humor a lot in classes and outside of classes. I tend to have a sarcastic style and the students can throw it back at me. Hopefully there aren't any consequences. Students usually know when I'm serious.

Many students have seen me come to tears. They've seen me intense. I just don't worry about it too much. In fact, I think these emotions help to balance power in the relationship. For example, in an undergraduate class, I teach students how to paraphrase, be empathic, and listen. In a typical activity, there are eight students sitting in a circle, and I'm their "client." The students will take turns responding to me. I'll say something, then one student responds; I say something else, then the next student responds. I never think about what I'm going to talk about ahead of time—I just don't. One day I ended up talking about my brother, who died two years ago. Obviously it's very powerful for me. The students, especially as undergraduates, were very surprised to hear their professor talk about something so personal. But they did such a beautiful job. They were effective in part because I gave them something real to grab hold of. They respected my experience, and they honored it by attending to it—exactly the skills we were studying. It was really tender. Without talking about it at any great length, they got a different sense of who I am outside of being a teacher. They saw me as human being.

Wednesday evenings are the highlight of my week. At 3:30 in the afternoon, my Practicum in Marriage and Family Therapy class (eight graduate students) loads up a university van with cameras, TV monitors, cables, etc. and heads to Cheyenne. In response to the emotional and psychological needs of families impacted by the war on terrorism and deployment, we deliver family counseling services for couples and families associated with the Wyoming Air and Army Guard. We literally become a mobile therapy clinic. As we drive to Cheyenne through the fog and snow, we address last minute needs such as session planning, working together as co-therapists, and how to best support each other with constructive feedback. The ride over serves as a time to center and connect before the whirlwind pace of the evening begins.

Upon our arrival, we look like a military unit on a mission as each person does her or his part in converting four unlikely rooms into a counseling clinic. As the night unfolds, we deliver up to nine sessions to couples and families trying to make the best of a difficult situation. Upon ending our last sessions at 8:45 PM, we disassemble everything we put together less than five hours prior and are back on the road in twenty minutes. During our return trip we process themes, discuss challenges, and highlight our successes. Throughout the evening we enter into serious discussions as well as playful bantering. Both dialogues equally bring us closer together as a group. At the end of the evening we say our good-byes knowing that we are going the extra mile it often takes to make a difference in the lives of others. While many of us struggle with the political direction of our country, we have chosen to collectively keep our beliefs in check as we focus on the bigger picture, nurturing relationships and supporting families. I am proud to be a member of this group.

Outside the Classroom

My office hours are posted. At the graduate level, it's almost meaningless because we're with each other so much of the time, especially when we're doing clinical work. I'm actually trying for the first time this year to be a little more strict with my office hours. I'm trying to fit people into office hours, and I think I'm getting a little bit better at it. Unfortunately, at the graduate level, everyone is always over-booked so when my office hours don't match with a student's schedule, we find a time that does work for all involved. They're very respectful. I close the door if I need to; otherwise it's open. For example, yesterday was supposed to be time for my work. A couple of students came in with a variety of issues, and we spent two or three hours talking. Schedules are meant to be flexible.

Because it's counseling, the students and I talk a lot about setting boundaries with clients. If you have clients calling you at home all the time, you're not setting clear boundaries. I try to model the same. I don't get very many calls at home. I get some from doctoral students, but usually I've told them, maybe at the crunch of their dissertation phase, "Call me at home." They're very respectful and sensitive to when it's okay and when it's not okay.

Occasionally I'll have social gatherings over at my house. But that's work related. Because graduate programs are so tight, I try to be cognizant of the problems caused by perceived favoritism. I think there's some reality to favoritism—some personalities get along with each other better than others. As far as personal relationships go, I try to keep those pretty clear. If I hook up with doctoral students outside of work, it's usually as a group where people aren't excluded.

A good deal of our time for both students and faculty is spent in our training clinic. As a means of both creating an enhanced professional atmosphere and facilitating group/program cohesion, we initiated the "Trading Spaces, Counseling Style" Project. This project is based on a TLC network production in which couples or families trade houses for a couple of days and remodel a room with limited funds. It was evident that we met the two basic requirements. Our clinic was in dire need of attention and we always have limited funds. With the financial support of the Wyoming Counseling Association, we were able to redesign three of our individual counseling rooms in a twenty-four hour period. On a Friday afternoon at 5:00, three teams (students, friends, partners, and faculty) went to work on their rooms. Each group had a "vision" for their room and $250 in cash. The rules were simple. They could not see another group's room until the end of the twenty-four hour period, 4:00 the following day. The rest was up to them and their imaginations. Each group put their hearts and souls into their rooms. We laughed, made lots of mistakes together, learned how to do new things, and connected in a way that seldom happens in the confines of a classroom. In the end, the rooms beautifully expressed the individual personalities of each group. We were all very proud of our work. And we had it all on videotape. One of the participants volunteered to take the hours and hours of video and condense it into a twenty-minute show. This fall, we all gathered to watch the tape. It was a wonderful reminder of the importance of work, play, and connecting.

I wish there were enough money in the world for all of our students to go to conferences with us. Something different happens there as well. As a faculty member, I relax a little more. I'm not thinking about other things I have to do. I'm pretty playful with my students. I joke around; I give students a hard time; they give me a hard time. Nonetheless, doctoral students take themselves too seriously—I did when I was a doctoral student. Conferences make a difference. There we loosen up, we go out and about and we play, we do sessions together. Then when we come back, our relationships have grown. We interact on a different level—not so rigid and formal. Going to conferences makes us colleagues, especially at the doctoral level. When we give presentations together, go to receptions, or just hang out, grades, critiques, and hierarchies are not as prominent.

Counseling and academia don't always go together very well. In counseling, it's all about meeting people where they're at, helping them to go in a direction that feels good to them and is healthy. Academia means standards that the students have to meet. We're not too rigid on that, but all programs have cut-offs. When we talk about equality, I think about fairness and being congruent as a human being. It's challenging to be congruent in an academic environment. For one, academia doesn't always foster equality, especially outside my department. All of the rules aren't about being human. I find comfort in little pockets, and that's where I stay most of the time. Then I go to other events around campus. Everybody means well, but they're often not playing by the same set of rules.

Compared to counselor education, other disciplines and meetings and contexts for decision-making are less humanistic. Even within our department, you have to assign grades, and you have to decide if someone's appropriate for the field. Counseling is much more—and it's been criticized for this—about the process of change than the product of change. Academia is very much focused on product. When you just focus on the product, you miss so much. There's pressure—such as making dissertations look a certain way—that doesn't reflect the learning that's gone on. Sometimes I have to make myself care, make the superficial piece of it matter. At the master's level, most folks are going to be counselors; they're not going to go on for a PhD. If they have good hearts and souls, and if they really care about other human beings, they're going to do great things in this world. But you still have to grade their papers. These things are hard to balance.

I really enjoy when students graduate. It's actually easier to connect with students after they graduate than when they're here. A majority of our master's students stay in-state. We see them at conferences, which I enjoy. The counseling field is a small world, just like most professions. You can stay connected if you want. I can tell you honestly—at the master's level but especially at the doctoral level—it is the *coolest thing* to watch people graduate. It's wonderful to hood people, partly because I remember my graduations. They were all significant to me. I know what these students have been through. They walk across the stage, and their family and friends are there. You know how much ambivalence there is in the whole process. There's just so much up and down. Graduation is so sweet. At that point, though, it's not sweet to me as a faculty member. It's sweet as a person.

Fostering All Voices

The feedback I've gotten from students says, regardless of different opinions, they feel like their thoughts matter in class discussions. I work really hard at this. I make it clear when I'm giving them my personal opinion. When people take risks in class, I think I do a pretty good job of acknowledging that, of thanking them. I try to attend to them in a way that lets them know that who they are, what they're about, and what they're about to say are all important. Sometimes I'll pull students aside at the end of class, especially at the master's level where I think they really wonder whether they're doing well, and tell them how much I appreciate what they're saying.

Our courses involve a lot of discussion in class. I have twenty-five graduate students this semester in one of my classes. That's big for a counseling course. To minimize the potential negative impact of size, I structure the class into family groups. Whenever we're sharing experiences and thoughts that are sensitive in nature, I have them get into their family groups—the same five or six people throughout the semester. I bounce around, but I don't need to be privy to all of their conversations. When we're talking about issues that are more theoretical in nature, less personal, then we talk in the larger group. The students always have the option to share something from a small group, but it's not a requirement. When they give me their family-of-origin papers, I'm the only person who sees them.

I think I'm pretty good at helping voices come out with issues of gender. When I teach a couples therapy class, we talk about gender a lot—it's kind of built in. I think I know what it means to have a male voice in a predominantly female profession. Our numbers are probably eighty percent female and twenty percent male within the program. So I'm very cautious not to make gender-based jokes and statements. If I do, I'll make them about men. I think I can play around with the male stereotypes a little bit more than the female. With the male stereotypes, I have more latitude. It's understood.

Our male students experience some male bashing. In small classes, they may be the only male. Sometimes they feel they have to represent everything that any man has ever done. When there are a small number of men, I try to throw myself into the mix, using "we" language with the guys. On many levels males can feel vulnerable. They're in a counseling program made up predominantly of women, a world that's highly verbal, whereas men often times aren't as skilled at being verbal. This can be a good thing. Part of the training experience for white men is to feel vulnerable just a little more than they would outside the counselor-training experience. The majority of the people they'll work with are not going to be white males. We tend to enter into this practice with less experience feeling vulnerable and as such we need to monitor ourselves. I don't want to create this experience, but if the men in our program experience it, it's valuable. It gives them an empathic idea of how most of the world lives every day. They experience the minority position, even if for just a moment.

So I do okay with gender. My experience is that both women and men feel comfortable with who I am and how I structure the class. I do need to get better on issues of race, color, and ethnicity. The number of ethnic minority students in the program is pretty low, *maybe* ten percent. We do have a growing number of international students. Paying attention to ethnicity means for me, a white male from an upper-middle-class background with limited exposure, keeping it in the front of my brain more often. Being in Wyoming—and Nebraska was no different—it's easy to avoid conversations around ethnicity and race. The large majority of our students have limited exposure outside their own white ethnicity. In the theory class, I bring in a lot of case examples. Many of these examples, which we talk about and play with, I tweak from actual cases I worked with in other locations. Most of those are white. I try to bring in other cases or ask, "What would change if this family were Hispanic or African American?" When I have students doing clinical work with someone who is of a different race, I'm sensitive about including that in the conversation. But when it's not right there, sometimes it's still an afterthought for me. I'm not proud of that, but it's the truth—an area I need to improve.

Until recently I was making the assumption that socioeconomic class does not show up much in my program. Since class was not a negative factor in my life, I made the assumption that my students were of similar class backgrounds. Was I ever wrong! One of our students recently facilitated a powerful activity that physically demonstrated how class was and is the single largest difference among our students. At the end of the activity we were stretched out across Prexy's pasture. Those with the most economic opportunities were at the front of the pack while those with fewer opportunities were at the back. While I was not surprised that I had a lot of breaks in my life, it was clear that many of our students have not had these opportunities. I was both embarrassed to be so unaware and proud to be in a group of individuals of such great strengths.

This experience brings to mind the importance of having diversity as an integral component of our programs here at UW. I believe that, especially in frontier areas such as Wyoming, courses exploring culture, diversity, oppression, and prejudice need to be both separate courses and woven into most (if not all) courses. Deborah McGriff teaches our multicultural counseling class. She is amazing on issues of diversity and multiculturalism. It helps me to know that our students get something very powerful from her class. But it doesn't mean I'm off the hook.

I brought the National Coalition Building Institute, a diversity model, to campus after Matthew Shepard was killed. Ten of us from around campus went away for training in 1998, and we offered a training here on campus. It's a diversity model where you lead workshops around issues of race, culture, gender, but it's experiential—people are actually having conversations, talking about the stereotypes they have in their heads. It's a pretty good workshop. I stayed with it because I needed practice having those conversations. I do better with a little structure, like when the team would teach workshops to students or have conversations among ourselves about the issues on campus. We had a team for about three years, but we decided to let it go because we were struggling with funding. Now, as a next step, it would be good for me to take an African American studies

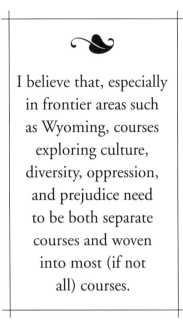

I believe that, especially in frontier areas such as Wyoming, courses exploring culture, diversity, oppression, and prejudice need to be both separate courses and woven into most (if not all) courses.

class. I hope that my students see me as open and approachable on issues of diversity and culture. I hope they know I'm willing to consider these issues, but also know I'm not an expert, which is fine by me. I'm willing to talk about tough things and be awkward while I'm doing so.

Role Models

I think of one person in particular as a role model from my master's and doctoral training at the University of Northern Colorado, David Gonzalez. He probably does not know I think of him in this way, but that's part of the nature of it. I worked with him during my practicum training for my master's degree. In counseling we talk about the importance of being genuine. He was such a person. He was the same with a client as he was as a supervisor, a teacher, or a person walking across campus. Genuine, sensitive, caring. These are the qualities we talk a lot about in humanistic models of counseling: being available and congruent. David modeled these qualities for me. He also gave me the most powerful assignment of my academic career. In his Psychology of Prejudice course, we were required to initiate and maintain a relationship with an individual from a group that we had a prejudice against. This experience taught me two things that I hope to never forget. First, we all have biases and prejudices. Second, my stereotypes and fears have the ability to keep me in a box. While I might feel safe in my box, there is a limited amount of oxygen in my box, so I need to get out and breathe some fresh air from time to time.

When I think about role modeling, going to conferences and presenting comes to mind. There's also the modeling about seeing clients of my own from time to time. This shows students what it's like to be professional in the field. Especially at the doctoral level, I'm trying to do more of that. But those are the job requirements, not the more important piece. The more important piece, which I hope I role model, is that students see a sense of who I am as a human being struggling to be the person I hope to some day become. They need to figure out who that is for themselves. I think I role model that I struggle. I don't know it all. When I teach the couples class, I talk about Carol and me. With her permission, I talk about Carol, I talk about Katie, my daughter. I talk about these normal things—being in love and maintaining a marriage and trying to be a parent.

Epilogue

Counselor education is a wonderful profession. But it's selfish in many ways. I can tell you honestly (and I tell students this—I'm not trying to brag) that I wouldn't be who I am as a father, who I am as husband—even with all the screw-ups—who I am as a son and a friend, if I hadn't gotten into this profession. I started out in architecture. But something drew me to counseling in a bigger way. I'm much better for it. I would have been academically strong, intelligent, in whatever field. But this field has helped me to be more honest with myself. I think that's probably the most important role modeling.

Teaching from the Other Side

Dominic Martinez
Minority Student Recruitment

I came to the University of Wyoming as a freshman in 1993. I wanted to become a high school history teacher. After earning my degree, I left for a short period to do a number of different things. I substitute taught a little bit, and I traveled with the Low Rider Show, a Mexican American car show and concert. Then I came back to Laramie with the idea of getting this job. I have been the coordinator of minority student recruitment for three years. I am working on a master's degree in

Dominic teaches his students about more than their cultures and their rights. He teaches them about life. He encourages his students' dreams, and he challenges them to encourage others' dreams as well. Dominic's life is about giving back. There is no distinction between his professional life. Dominic is constantly in search of opportunities to promote change. That is why his students never forget him. He might start out as a teacher to his students, but in the end he becomes more of a family member.

—Student nominator

counselor education. I teach one of the University Studies courses in a FIG (a freshman interest group) that focuses on cultural diversity. In the summer, I work with several programs that bring high school students to campus.

In this project, I would like to learn more about the way I teach. Also, I would like to find out what other teachers are doing, what they're doing to warm up that chill and make students feel as though they can speak out in their classrooms. That's what's really important in teaching.

The Context of Work with Students

My job is based on the idea of motivating students, getting them involved, making them feel like it's possible to obtain an education. A lot of these students have parents who haven't even graduated from high school, so they're trying to build a relationship with higher education. I go to schools, community events, and churches. I visit students at their houses. I travel throughout the U.S.: Chicago to Las Vegas, L.A. to Montana, talking with students about the University of Wyoming but more importantly about why education is important. I always quote Malcolm X: "Education is our passport to the future; for tomorrow belongs to the people who prepare for it today." I talk a lot about what that means. Then I give the whole University of Wyoming spiel about what we can do for students.

Three years ago, Kathy Evertz asked me to teach University Studies 1000. I have an education background, so I was kind of excited, but I wanted to take a different approach. I wanted to deal with diversity, meaning women, ethnic minorities, and LGBTA issues. Last fall, which was the second time I taught the class, I thought, Why not recruit ethnic minorities throughout Wyoming, throughout Colorado to take my class? This past year I also helped develop a FIG called Exploring Multi-culturalism: Making Visible the Invisible. And I tied my class to this FIG. In a FIG—a freshmen interest group—the students live on the same floor and they have the same RA. The RA and I work together to create a living environment and activities outside the classroom that are coherent with the classroom. We watch movies, eat dinners, and go on road trips. Two other courses are involved—Introduction to Religion and Cultural Diversity in America, which is an American Studies course. In my class, we focus on being leaders—power and what you can do with it. We do community service, we read books, we read articles. We talk about what it means to be different—why it's good to be different but at the same time why it's good to take those differences and try to find the similarities in them. We watch *The Breakfast Club* and talk about how these students are totally different when they meet each other, but by the end of the day, they leave as one.

To let students know about the FIG, the first thing I do is send an invitation to every ethnic minority student who is accepted to the university. The next thing I do is set up a booth during orientation. I tell students, if you're interested in multiculturalism, there's this FIG you can sign up for. Also, the FIG program sends out a brochure with all of the different FIGs students can choose from. This next year our FIG will be called The American Dream: Cultural Diversity in the Twenty-First Century. It will involve the same classes: Introduction to Religion, Cultural Diversity, and my University Studies class. We work together so that I can tie all of the class topics together in FIG activities. Some of the projects in the Cultural Diversity class, for example, include a big project on cultural diversity in food. At the end, the students make all this great food.

I continue to see the students I've recruited after they're here. I'm on the board of directors for MSLI (Minority Student Leadership Initiative), which was started in 1996–1997. It's a mentoring program for incoming freshmen. I'm in charge of identifying these students and then matching them up with their student and staff or faculty mentors. I also recruit faculty and staff. I send an email out to people I think would be good. Donna Amstutz is a mentor; Sally Steadman is one. Sally's on our committee, too. It's all volunteer. People like that make it what it is. They don't even get service credit.

The difference between the MSLI faculty or staff mentor and the academic adviser is that the mentor is someone who has the same interests as the student. Hobby-type interests. They'll do a number of things together on or off campus—cultural events, dinner. The mentor becomes a parent away from home. It varies what the different faculty or staff mentor does, but they discuss general concerns and build a relationship. The student mentor does something similar—plays the big-brother, big-sister role, encourages them to get involved, and helps them fill out scholarship applications. Our goal is to have the mentors and mentees meet at least twice a month. And once a month on a Sunday the entire group gets together for food and a speaker, for example, someone from the student exchange program or AWARE's spring break safety program. We give prizes out, get the students together, laugh.

I'm a mentor myself; I have two mentees. One's from Cheyenne and the other is from Green River. They're both young women, so they always want to do female things. A couple of weeks ago, we got massages, pedicures, manicures. I took them to a Broncos game.

It was all started by James C. Hurst. After Jason Thompson and I were student body president and vice president, Dr. Hurst realized that it had taken too long—a hundred years—to have the first black and Mexican president and vice president. That was 1996–1997. Dr. Hurst felt there was a need to develop leadership among freshmen. Since then, we have had Lisa Esquibel, Jesus Rios, and Warnell Brooks—all student leaders who have gone through our program. We have seven ethnic minority senators this year who went through MSLI. What we've done seems to help.

MSLI is in its fourth year. We have twenty-five mentees this year—freshmen who came in during fall 2001. Our retention rates are a lot higher than the university's. We're at 86–90 percent retention. The freshmen student body at large is at about 70–80 percent. Out of twenty-five, twenty-three are on the honor roll. We have a student worker in this office who deals only with MSLI students. She emails them, makes sure they're doing okay, does the evaluations. All of this happens with a budget of $1,100 a year. A lot of us on the committee go into our own pockets. We've always paid for dinner. My mentees and I are going to a concert in May. I want to give them something that I didn't have as a freshman.

I also have a recruitment team of students. They're called La Junta, which means "the gathering." It includes two students from every ethnic group: Asian American, American Indian, African American, and Mexican American, or Hispanic, Chicano. We meet in my office every Friday at 3:00, and we talk about what we can do. These students go out to high schools, write letters, send emails; they're actively involved in recruiting other students. It's all volunteer. In addition to these students, I have recruited five students who work with me through work study.

I am the adviser for the United Multicultural Council. We meet every week at 5:00 until about 7:00 and talk about issues on campus and how we're going to change them. It's just students; I'm the only staff person. My evenings are packed with student activities outside of recruiting. Then I also own a DJ company that employs students I recruit.

My summers are packed with summer programs, for example the Daniels Fund Summer Prep and Scholarship Program, which is for low-income students in the state of Wyoming. They spend a week with us, working on essay writing, financial aid forms, computer work, study skills, etiquette. We talk to them about being different. We talk about the three Ps, pride, progress, and power: pride within yourself; progress, always trying to reach education—go for whatever you can, never stay in one spot; and power to control your own destiny. They're juniors in high school—in the summer after their junior year. If they're awarded one of the scholarships through the Daniels Fund, which is in Sheridan, they have a full ride to go to any college they want. Daniels pays for everything.

The other summer program I run is the Chicano Studies Summer Seminar. We take high school aged students from throughout the U.S. They come for a week of intense Chicano Studies—Chicano history, Chicano literature, Chicano film, poetry. We go camping, bring in storytellers, touch on the American Indian aspects of life.

I'm also a seminar leader for the High School Institute, which is aimed at sophomores in Wyoming. They go to classes during the day, classes that represent extracurricular interests, not pure academics. In the evening, they go to a seminar. The students call it therapy, but it's not really therapy. About eleven students and I sit around every night for an hour-and-a-half and talk about issues. Last year, a student talked about coming out of the closet during the seminar. It's set up so that students can say anything and it doesn't leave the room.

The focus is to get the students comfortable being away from home—it's a three-week program—and to let the students start networking with others throughout the state. It's so funny to see these students the first day they get here. They're really quiet; they don't know each other. By the last day, they're crying and saying, "I promise I'll contact you everyday." I'm probably one of the few people who gets to see the students on a monthly basis, because I travel to some of their high schools. I get to see all the students who come through the summer programs. And then when they come here, they're familiar with somebody; they know there's going to be someone they know.

I also work with the UDOC program, which is a program for a combination of first-generation, low-income, ethnic minority, rural, and female students who come for seven weeks of pre-med classes like human anatomy and molecular biology. They're taught at a college level. They have to write a fifteen-page essay that gets published in a booklet. And they do rotations; they have to shadow doctors somewhere in the state—even going through cadaver labs. The first year I did this, it was all women. Last year, there were two men. So I've had to learn a lot about gender issues. That first year made me start to think about gender—women aren't being taught at the same level as men, elementary through high school. Women are considered secondary to men. Some of these females will come into this program and say, "Well, I think I want to be a nurse." And we'll ask them, "Why do you want to be a nurse?" "Well, most women are nurses." "No, you're better than that. Nursing is a good field, but why not be a doctor?"

We had our first graduating class—students graduating from pre-med who went through the UDOC program—two years ago. We have some who are in medical school right now, and they're going to be doctors. That's the cool thing. I'm amazed to see their growth. One student is now in our WWAMI program. When she came to UDOC, she didn't even think she was smart enough to be in the sciences, to be in math. She's been in the program for five and a half years now, and next year she'll go to Washington to do her second year of medical school. As a high school student, she had a little trouble. She was really timid. But by the time she started the undergrad degree, she had the foundation to think, I've already taken human anatomy here; I've already taken molecular biology. I know these professors. I'm not scared anymore to raise my hand and say, "I don't understand." Now she's going to medical school, which is kind of cool.

Sometimes I don't like this job because I feel I don't have my own life. But other times I think, if I wasn't doing it, who else would? Since I've started work, I have never been able to take time off. I'm leaving tomorrow for my first vacation. When I'm on the road recruiting, I'm always on my email, or the cell phone is ringing off the hook. At times, I want to leave Laramie to see if I can help others in different areas.

Teaching to the Whole Person

My main focus is to provide a support system for students who are ethnic minority. I recruit them, so I feel responsible. And I'm not just recruiting the students; I'm recruiting the parents, the grandparents, the community. I'll be woken up by the phone at night—parents calling to find out where their child is. I'm out at midnight, going through the Cowboy bar, looking for their son or daughter. I give my parents a stack of business cards. People in the community are always asking my parents, "Can you tell Dominic I have a daughter (or a son or a grandchild) coming up to college?" or "There's this neighbor kid who's minority I think could go to college. Could your son call him?"

Sometimes students end up living with me for a while because they arrive before the residence halls open. Or they get kicked out of the halls for stupid reasons. They stay with me until they figure out the next step.

> My main focus is to provide a support system for students who are ethnic minority. I recruit them, so I feel responsible. And I'm not just recruiting the students; I'm recruiting the parents, the grandparents, the community.

I can tell if someone is in trouble. It's on their face; they're slumped over. I know most of the people who work with me like family. In class, I can tell that something's wrong by the way a student speaks. I'll pull that person over and say, "Hey, you know what? I know you may not want to talk with me, but I'm here in case you want to talk. You can call me at home or at work. If you want to go for a soda or go for dinner, you know I'm here." At the end of emails to my students, I write, "Your brother." I want them to know I'm their brother. I'll bend over backward. I had a student who needed to get his green card renewed. His parents couldn't come up to get him, so I took him down there; we sat in Denver for eight hours. I took a day off so we could do that. I'll do those things to make sure students can succeed.

Above the Office of Student Life, there's a sign that says, "Our mission, your success." That's what I tell my students. No matter what we have to do, we'll do it to help you succeed: if we need to get you a tutor, if you need to borrow $20, if you need books. Students know they can come to me. A student needed to borrow my truck to go home for spring break; I said, "Take it." Little things add up.

The Teacher-Student Relationship: Negotiating Power

Inside the Classroom

My class is never in the same place. I've never had a class in the same room from week to week. University Studies assigns me a room, and we'll meet there the first day. But after that, we meet at Winger's, other restaurants, at the Union, the residence halls. I have to sit behind a desk, or in a car or on a plane, and I get tired of that. When I was a freshman, I hated some of these classrooms. So I told myself, I want to be different. I want my students to feel comfortable. When we do meet in the regular classroom, I tell students to sit on their desks, sit on the floor, get a couple of chairs, and put them together. I'll sit up front on top of the desk. That's how we'll talk. I also like to pull everyone into a circle.

The students always come up with suggestions for places to meet, and that shows me they like the fact that we move around. I ask for suggestions, and they're always saying, "Why not this, Why don't we go here?" For the second week of class, I tell the students to meet me in my office in the Visitor's Center. We'll sit out here on the couches. I show them my office and say, "This is your office too. Use it whenever you'd like to." I try to make an open environment with them. I tell them, "There's going to be a time when I call on you to help me out." And there are plenty of times when they step forward to help with my recruitment activities or my University Studies FIG group.

I offered a shadow day, which was called Shadow of Success, in which high school ethnic minority students from throughout the state of Wyoming visited campus. I needed places for these students to stay. Everyone in my University Studies class said they'd let someone stay in their room. In some instances, the host students were Caucasian, but others were Hispanic or American Indian, and the visiting students got to meet them and see that different culture.

Students are aware that they're being graded, and they're worried about having to leave because they won't make the grades. The first day,

I tell them, "You're all starting off with As. But you might drop that A. When I ask for work, you get that work in. If you don't show up to class, your A is affected." That tells them it's their responsibility. I use the quotation from Thomas S. Monson that says, "Decisions determine destiny." And I talk with the students about how the decisions they make will determine who they're going to be and what they end up doing. I talk a lot about that the first day of class.

At the same time, I tell the students I want them to grade me. The students grade me throughout the semester. If they feel like it, they'll write to me as a group: "We like what you did today" or "We don't like what we did; maybe we could try it another way." I complete the same writing assignments that I ask them to do. I ask the students to write journals; they have to send them to each other. I'll write a journal and share it with them. These students come with so many different perspectives on life, I'm learning more from the students than they'll ever learn from me.

Class is set up with leadership, like a council. If the class wants to assign a class president, that person will collect all of the papers. Then I have a couple of student leaders who work with me. They'll ask me to leave the room, or they'll meet with the other students outside of class—they all live on the same floor—and then they'll send me feedback. I tell them they can say anything—you can cuss, you can cry, you can laugh, you can be pissed off. If you want to grab a chair and slam it on the ground, that's fine. That's how we're going to teach. We're going to deal with the issues that come up. Everything is a learning experience.

One of the students who nominated me for this project wasn't even in my class. But he attended every class meeting, because he'd heard from one of the students, "Hey, this is a different class." I always have five to ten people who aren't registered for the class but show up. They're not even getting credit. But they turn in journals and take part in the class project.

Professors often ask me to come into their classrooms and talk about diversity. I talk about making visible the invisible. I use a soccer ball. I ask them to write a description of the ball—it's round; it's white. Then I have them lay down and close their eyes, and I talk to them. I read some poetry. I say, "I'm invisible, understand, simply because people refuse to see me." We talk about what that means. Then I ask them to open their eyes and re-see the ball. Become the ball. Talk to the ball. Listen to the ball. It has a history. Then students will write about what they see now that they didn't see on the first look. I love to make assumptions about students—that's a Sorority Girl; that's Mr. Athlete, Mr. Buff. And I confess it: "This is what I think of you. What do you think about me?" Then we talk about how we're more than our outer appearance.

Titles affect the student-teacher relationship as much as appearances do. Donna Amstutz talks about this. Some of her students call her Doctor; some call her Donna. I think that's the approach I take. I want students to feel comfortable enough to say whatever they want. When you start throwing titles in there, that's when the comfort disappears. A lot of professors will walk in and say, "I'm Professor so-and-so" or "I'm Dr. so-and-so." What are they communicating with these statements? I'm not a professor. Sometimes I think I don't teach, that I'm just there to have a conversation. Sometimes I don't even look at them as students. I see them as colleagues. We sit together and discuss issues.

When Kathy first asked me to teach, I said, "But I'm not a professor." She continues to ask, and the teaching is what I love about my job. If I picked something about work that made me feel important, made me feel good, it would be the teaching. That's the way I approach recruiting. I don't say, "The University of Wyoming was built in 1886." I'll talk instead about why it's important to go to school. I tell students I don't care where they go; I don't care whether they go to the University of Wyoming. I care that they get an education. I'll tell them why I got an education and what it's done for me.

I've thought about going back and teaching high school. But I'm not sure I want to be in front of the classroom every single day. I like the idea of traveling in the teaching capacity. I teach about college. I really enjoy working with the students. They make me feel young. There are some who aren't as experienced, who aren't as world-wise as others, but there are some who are really experienced, even in working with students, and I learn a lot from them.

Outside the Classroom

My office is open to students. Students tend to come in here a lot. I keep my refrigerator stocked with sodas and treats and candies. I have a microwave; students come in here to eat. They use the computers. There's a fax machine if they need things faxed; a telephone if they need to call home. They come in and hang out at least two or three times a week.

How I handle power in recruiting varies from day to day. It depends on the situation. Maybe we're not going to be able to admit someone. If it's a student I know, I always ask to be the one to let that person know. Instead of sending a letter, I'll call the student. That's more personal than getting this letter, which you have to read over and over. I try to talk to him or her about it and say, "I'm not going to give up on you." I'll suggest different avenues: "Why don't we get you started with community college? Why don't you write a letter to the director of the program? Why don't you get letters of recommendation?" A lot of times, I'll call people who have worked with these students and ask them what they know. Then I'll tell these students, "I'm going to work my hardest to build a case for you, but you have to meet me half way." And when they are eventually accepted, I say, "I bent over backwards; now you have to prove to me that you can do this—don't make my word, my rep, get destroyed."

I've had to turn away some of my cousins and my best friends' brothers and sisters. My boss keeps me in the loop, so I can call right away to say, "It looks like you're not going to get in." But then I try to keep the possibilities open. I'll continue talking to them if, for example, they go to community college. I'll call and ask how it's going. But I also tell them I'm not going to do it on my own.

The students who work with me know what's going on in my office. I think I'm one of the few employers who shows students the budget. I'll tell them, "We have this program coming up called I'm Going to College; it's for elementary students. I've organized it for two years; I'm turning it over to you. You guys plan it, get the speakers, order the food, send out the letters to the schools." My student workers tell me that they like this, that it makes them feel powerful.

At the beginning of the semester, I show the student workers a list of everything that has to be done that term. I tell them we'll meet every Monday at 3:00. For these meetings, we don't check off items from an agenda. I try to make it more fun. I have a big foam hat. If someone comes in angry, that person has to wear the hat. Or if everyone is angry, we'll go play football outside. They laugh at me and say, "We didn't know you could run." It's cool just to let the students know you're human. I have some students who work for me who say, "It feels like we don't even work." But we get a lot of things done.

When we first learned that we would have the Daniels Program, the university wanted to hire two staff to run it. I asked to hire a student instead. The program is run by myself and one student. She's the assistant director. Who could be an assistant director as a student? She has to give presentations on the program in Denver, in Utah, in New Mexico. I try to hire students who are really quiet but have that energy. I can see it in their eyes—these students have the desire.

I might use intuition. I was trying to explain this the other day to some people who were asking, "How do you get these students who end up being some of the best leaders on campus?" I just get a feeling around them. Some of these students grew up with single parents or didn't even grow up with parents. Adrian Molina, for example, is one of the top students on this campus. He writes, he publishes poetry, he does all of this stuff. When I was doing my student teaching, Adrian was a junior in high school and needed a place to live. I told him to move in with me. He moved in with me his senior year. At the end of the year I was done student teaching and moved back to Laramie. He moved with me. I kind of raised this kid. I got a feeling from him. Some of the other students I've hired—I just got a feeling from them.

Fostering All Voices

I don't concentrate as much in my work on gender as I do on social issues. But I'd like to try to do more. My last University Studies class included two males and ten females. We talked a lot about the differences and similarities—what each sex liked and disliked about the other. And we talked about date rape and violence. But I don't know the figures on what women are getting paid compared to men, the number of women going to college compared to men—I don't know those issues. But I would like to learn more.

All my close friends are females. We laugh about it—I feel like I'm one of the girls. They'll tell me, "Oh, that guy's so cute; what do you think?" And I'll say, "Well, he looks really good in those jeans." Having been raised by my mom and my sisters, I'm aware of the things girls think about—colors and so on. And I don't like to get dirty. I'd rather vacuum than go out and mow the lawn. My dad told me something that sticks with me: "Treat women the way you'd want someone to treat your mom and your sisters." That has affected me; no one can imagine their mom being treated like crap.

I concentrate a lot on race. The students and I talk about differences; we talk about stereotypes. We talk about tolerance. I don't like that word, but we talk about tolerance. We do a lot of critical thinking, working on questions like, Why do people treat each other like they do? We try to get to the center of racism, which is fear. I ask the students, "Tell me the names you've been called growing up." And then I ask them what they have called other people. The second list is always a lot longer. We also talk about pay structure: Why are minorities getting paid less than the majority? Why is it important to help ethnic minorities seek education? We'll talk about affirmative action.

I don't think there is equal opportunity for students of color, not even at the elementary or junior high level. A lot of people don't take that into consideration. I've talked with people who say, "I pulled myself up by my boot straps. Why can't ethnic minorities do that? I'm tired of hearing about your minority scholarships. We're all equal. It says that in the Constitution. Slavery ended a long time ago. The American Indian thing ended a long time ago. The Mexican American thing ended a long time ago. Let's just deal with it and get over it." But institutional racism is still there, no matter where you go. There is institutional racism here at the University of Wyoming.

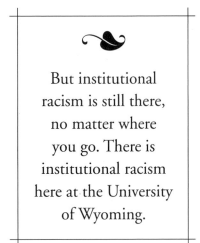

But institutional racism is still there, no matter where you go. There is institutional racism here at the University of Wyoming.

When I was student teaching, some teachers would say in the teachers' lounge, "That student's going to be in jail." These were assumptions about the student's future based on his or her race. A while back I wrote a paper called "The 14-Year-Old Chicano" about my first day of high school, when I was talking with the guidance counselor, trying to work out my schedule. I told the counselor I wanted to take chemistry and algebra. She turned to me and said, "Why don't you take automotives? Mechanics make $14 an hour." She was pushing students of color toward skilled work, the technical fields, instead of the sciences. In history class the teacher talked about all of these great men. None of them were Martinez, Sanchez, Garcia, Cruz. In high school, I really got into Malcolm X. It was Black History Month, and the history teacher covered, in one day, Martin Luther King: "Martin Luther King was a great man, we loved him, and he did great things." Then he said, "And there was this Malcolm X guy, but he hated everyone who wasn't black, so we're not going to talk about him." I went home that day and asked my mom if she would buy me the autobiography of Malcolm X. I started reading about him, and my life changed. I started copying the dictionary like him. I started reading everything I could get my hands on.

Students know—from my passion—what my feelings on these issues are. I let students know where I stand on issues right when we start talking. But I always tell them, "Hey, if you disagree with me, you may be able to change my mind. I want you to speak up. I want you to be that student who says, 'Dominic, I disagree with you.'" I've had students do that, and my ideas have changed a lot.

I want students to see the other side. If my daughter or son would come home drunk or high, I would make them volunteer at a clinic; I would take them to an AA meeting. I would want them to see what drug use can lead up to. I was at Elmer Lovejoy's just last week, and a few of us were talking about Democrats and Republicans. Someone asked, "Who here is Democrat?" I raised my hand, and so did an Asian American gentleman. A white gentleman at another table said, "It's f'ing typical for a f'ing minority to be Democrat." I just sat there. But he came over and joined us. He continued, "I'm tired of your scholarships." I tried to explain to him where I stand. "I'm cool with what you believe, but this is my opinion, and that's what this country is all about—we're entitled to our opinions." "Well you say you're Mexican American; you should be American." I said, "No, I'm Mexican American." "Well then go back to Mexico." So I said, "Well, then, go back to Italy."

One of my activities requires students to talk with someone who is very different from them. You have to find someone who is of a different race, sex, and religion than yourself. You introduce yourself, ask if you can eat lunch together. You sit and talk with them for two hours. Then you have to write a report about what you've learned, about that other person's perspective and background. That gets students to step out of their comfort zone. Some of the students say they won't do it. But I tell them, "I'll flunk you; you have to do it. I'll flunk you all." Usually they come back and say, "It was so cool. I met this person. I learned so much." I tell them, "That's what life's about. You'll learn so much more from people than what you'll ever learn from books." Then for the rest of the semester—every two weeks—they have to go out and meet someone else, another person who is different from them. I often make this assignment when I visit classes to talk about diversity. Professors send me email saying, "It was one of the coolest assignments." It gets people to start talking to each other.

A book by Beverly Tatum is entitled, *Why Are All of the Black Kids Sitting Together in the Cafeteria?* The answer is comfort zone. If you walk through the breezeway in the Union, you'll see all of the black students sitting together, all of the Mexican Americans sitting together. We fear the unknown. Students will argue, "Well, how do you approach someone and say, 'Tell me about your race?'" That's how you approach them! You don't have a script. Walk up to them and say, "I know this is weird, but I'm doing an assignment, and I would like to talk with you about who you are." It works.

My goal is to get this campus to think, to look at the big picture. The only way we can succeed is if we know each other. When it comes to race, I don't think minorities need to know more about diversity. We already know how to be the minority. We know how to be the majority, too; we have to live in two worlds. My goal is to reach out to students who aren't in the minority.

In my FIG this year, I had two ethnic minorities out of twelve. There are students who want to learn about these issues. Last year when I taught University Studies, I had all minority students but one. That student came to me and said, "Now I know what it's like to be a minority." Even though I recruit for minority students, not that many of them will sign up for my University Studies class. They say, "I've already dealt with it," which is fine. We talk a lot about race. But we also talk about students, in general, and how people treat them in this community because they're young.

Channel 2 news interviewed me a while back. They asked me why it's important for ethnic minority students to attend UW. I said, "Well, why isn't it? This is what the real world looks like. The state of Wyoming. If you go into major businesses and schools—any place where work requires a college degree—the majority is white. You have to learn how to work in this environment. I work at the University of Wyoming, and I know who I see when I sit down at staff meetings. It's old white men. Now, occasionally, I see a woman. On campus our ethnic minority population is about eight or nine percent. But look at your faculty and staff. Look at the administrators. How many ethnic minorities do you see there? We're not where we should be. And America isn't where it should be."

That's what I mean when I talk with the students about social justice. The good-old-boy system tells you who will get the job. I'm the coordinator of minority student recruitment, and I don't operate that way. If any student needs help, I'll give it to them: white, black, orange, purple. My classes are made up mostly of white students. It's weird for them to have to talk about race. That's not a comfortable thing to talk about.

Income level comes up in class, too. You don't have to be ethnic minority to be treated like crap. I know some poor Caucasian students are treated like dirt. Who do those students end up being friends with? The ethnic minorities. They have an understanding.

I knew a student whose name was Leif when I was doing my student teaching at Rawlins High School. All the teachers said they'd given up on him. Well, I put all my energy into working with him. I wanted him to feel like he could do anything. The day I left—he wore the same outfit the entire semester, the same clothes, the same jacket—he tore off a button, gave it to me, and said, "You're the only person who has ever given me a chance." I still have that button. It's on my book cabinet at my house.

People think things are balanced, but they're not. People who have the money and own the businesses say there's nothing wrong. I want to say, "Come with me for a week. Let me take you to California. Let me take you to *Wyoming*. Let me take you to Jackson and show you how Mexican immigrants work and where they live. I've slept on their floors. I've eaten dinner at their houses. I've gone to church with them. Many of these people are the best people you'll meet. They don't complain. This life is all they've known, and that's what they think they're good enough for."

Someone wrote, "How can we possibly bring out the best in our children if we won't bring out the best in ourselves?" I agree with that. I've taken a lot of classes on this campus, but I only thought of one when this project asked for nominations: Deborah McGriff. I'm in her class this semester in counselor education. She is amazing. I couldn't think of anyone else. I had teachers help me when I was in a jam but none who made me want to become a different person. It's a good school; I love the University of Wyoming, but there's some work to be done.

Role Models

My mom influenced me. At a very young age, she made it clear I could do whatever I wanted. She challenged me to be different, not to do things just because my friends did them. That's what I try to do with my students. There were times I went without friends. But I always had my mom. My dad, too: I have never met a man who has worked so hard to get what he has. He didn't always understand what school was about, but he always made sure that we had the financial backing to go to school if we wanted. They sacrificed a lot to make sure I got where I am now. I'm the only one of my brothers and sisters to go to college.

When it comes to teaching, my favorite role model is Marty Miyamoto. He was my biology teacher. I don't like science, never have, but he had us do hands-on work, and he showed us how scientific concepts affect our lives. He made me feel good about myself. When other teachers told me I wouldn't make it, he would always challenge me. One time, when I was really down about school, he pushed me up against the wall and said, "Do something about it. You're the only one who can do something about it." To this day, I owe a lot to that man.

I don't know if I look at myself as a role model. I'm not sure I want to be one. You don't have a life; if you do something wrong, it taints the students' image of you. But at the same time, I think students do look up to me. I try not to be their role model but their family member— someone who cares about them. A lot of students will say, "Well, Michael Jordan is my role model." But you don't get to interact with people like that on a daily basis. I would rather be a stable person in students' lives; I'd rather be there for them.

When I was in high school, I didn't have any Mexican American teachers. Or African American. I had one Asian American, Marty Miyamoto. He was a role model, but he wasn't even my own race. The people that were my race? They were the ones serving the food or mopping the floors. So that tells me, I can never get any better than this. It starts playing tricks with your mind: I don't see myself teaching; I don't see myself being a doctor. And that's something that I'm trying to fight. Being a janitor and being a cafeteria worker are great professions. My mom served food in the cafeteria when I was little. Construction, picking fruit—those are the jobs that make America. But at the same time, I tell students, "We need you in the sciences. We need you in politics, engineering, medicine." I'm challenging them.

Epilogue

I'll go into high schools, and I'll lift up a $20 bill. I'll ask the students, "Who wants this $20 bill?" Everyone starts yelling. I tell them the first person who can name ten ethnic minority American leaders gets the $20. No one has ever done it. I'll tear it in half and point out that money isn't anything if you don't have the education to back it up. I talk about Cesar Chavez. I'll hand the $20 to the teacher and say, "You can tape that back together. When somebody can write you a report about ten ethnic minority American leaders, you give that to them." Students want to impress others with the nice car and the jewelry. But I remind them they can't take that with them.

I try to teach the way I would like to be taught. That goes a long way. That's when you're going to get students. That's when students will come to you and say, "Hey, I like what you did. You opened my mind." It's not about how you're grading; it's about how you can open their minds to something new.

Trust, Planned Obsolescence, and a Sense of Play

Mark Ritchie
Art: Printmaking and Drawing

I am originally from eastern Kansas and received a bachelor of fine arts from the University of Kansas before spending a year of study in Wales and Scotland. When I returned to the United States, I attended

Mr. Ritchie is an excellent facilitator of dialogue between the students in a class. In my experience, he has offered up dialogue between students of different ethnic backgrounds, sexual orientation, and ages to make them feel comfortable and to allow for others to realize that we are all on the same level, just with different backgrounds or lives. This atmosphere has allowed the students to explore more in-depth imagery, baring their souls to the class without fear of being snuffed for content. He has developed a very trusting environment in which I have grown three-fold in one year, compared to my earlier years of education elsewhere.

—Student nominator

Indiana University where I earned a master of fine arts. Before moving to Wyoming, I taught at several universities and colleges as a sabbatical replacement and as an adjunct faculty member. I also worked as an artist in residence in schools and prisons in Georgia. I am now an associate professor in the Department of Art at the University of Wyoming. My own work fuses drawing and printmaking in small works on paper. The most recent work is based on Asian folding screens and Islamic miniatures, especially in scale, flattened space, metaphorical landscape and animals, and inference of human presence.

I'm interested in this project because I want to learn approaches I can take back to my classroom. I would also like to learn things that don't necessarily translate to my classroom but that give me a better sense of what's going on in the university outside of my discipline. Also, I have one perspective based on my own history, my own background. I'm interested in the perspectives and backgrounds of other faculty. As a white guy in his late thirties, I'm going to have a different take on situations than a woman who's in her early fifties. It's a great setting to hear about these things first hand. I think it's good to be involved in this discussion.

The Context of Work with Students

This is my seventh year at UW. For the first four years, I taught beginning drawing in addition to the book arts and the printmaking classes, which consist primarily of upper division major students. The drawing class gave me time with freshmen—people whose lights were just coming on. They were just getting excited about learning. Now I deal almost exclusively with students finishing their undergraduate program. I have certain expectations about these students, and I know that most of the students have reached a certain place in their artistic growth—they're getting ready to deal with the next big thing, polishing off their undergraduate art careers. Occasionally, non-majors come through, but it's mostly the specific population of majors. Because the department is relatively small and because we work with the students frequently outside of the class, it's also a group of students I've gotten to know even before I have them in my classes. The leaders start to stand out as each class comes through the ranks.

I'm the adviser for the Student Art League as well. There I interact with people who are not in my classes, and I often have long-term conversations with students who may later be in one of my classes. I have the luxury of developing trust with a core group of students, a group that takes people in as they enter the program and lets others go as they graduate. You'll see a group that works together really well and then a group that's not so coherent.

The art students spend a lot of time together outside of class. Many apply for student studios, which are divided according to discipline and granted according to merit. It's almost like a freshman interest group, except that it's juniors and seniors. For instance, all of the painting students who have applied for and received studio space are working on their BFA portfolios in the same place—maybe five students. The same is true with the students in ceramics or printmaking. These groups of students share spaces and learn to practice working together. I sometimes end up in counseling situations that maybe I shouldn't be in, but I understand that I must address these problems or they'll create problems in the classroom. Often these conflicts are not important enough to need a counselor, but they need smoothing, mediating. I try to address issues that could harm the community of the classroom and the department.

But of course the community is richer when the students jump over those hurdles independently. My role is to interact just enough to keep the students on track and working together.

Teaching to the Whole Person

Not everybody has the luxury I have in a studio classroom of knowing students quite well. An example would be knowing students' socioeconomic issues that aren't immediately visible—teachers don't always know these things about their students. When you get to know the students, you often realize that much of what the students are doing in the classroom and even many of the issues beyond the classroom that are simply part of university life are new experiences for them. Rarely do students acknowledge any lack of experience or discomfort in new situations. For me, it's a little like an Arthurian legend: they have to ask the right questions at the right time or they have to go on a mighty quest. The first generation students in particular often do not know what questions to ask. They often do not know their options. I need to create an atmosphere that allows them to ask questions or allows me to ask the right questions of each student at the right time. I will steer a conversation in a direction that may help them to ask about careers or to address anxieties. Advising is a great time for this, but so much of what should happen during advising doesn't happen in a fifteen-minute advising session. It happens when you help students with a project or help them apply for a scholarship. Trust comes first. From there, they can ask you the question so *you* can ask them the right questions to get to know them.

Working with small classes and classes that meet for a few hours, I have a level of interaction that you don't have in a room with sixty people in an hour-long lecture. There you have to assume that among that group of sixty there are socioeconomic issues and issues of sexuality, race, and gender. Nobody wears a sign that tells you about their identities. Or generally they don't. You only get what is revealed or obvious. In contrast, I often know the partners of my students and meet their families. Issues of race or socioeconomic issues that may not be apparent are often revealed when students discuss their work with me informally. When comments are made in an in-class conversation or during a critique of student work that are potentially damaging, I know who's being hurt and how. In a large classroom, you can only assume there might be somebody being hurt. Because I know who is affected, I often know how best to address the situation in that moment. I can tailor the classroom experience, and the issues we confront, for each student and each class. Different disciplines share a lot of the same issues surrounding equality, but what varies is how we're allowed to handle them. I am glad I am able to work with small groups of students in large blocks of time.

The Teacher-Student Relationship: Negotiating Power

Inside the Classroom

Power can be a really positive thing. I usually think of power as a negative concept. I try not to let the issue of power in determining a grade affect my interactions with students. But power is a good way to describe what's going on. I *do* have power in the classroom. I'm determining grades. I'm setting the agenda. There is power in that. I try to play it down with the students. I try to empower them by giving them ownership of the class. I see myself as a facilitator. Jokingly, I say I'm the divine mover of the class. I set it rolling and see where it goes. That's often my role—I determine when to introduce new material, when to ask specific questions of the students about their work, and how to structure evaluations and critiques based on the climate and issues of each class.

There are times when I need to take a very executive role. I speak to the students at length in a direct way. I do this when I see things breaking down. At these times I will place a big issue on the table that may have no definitive answer. It might be what the students will do next in life, issues of evaluation, questions about current issues in image making, the differences between art and craft, or an ethical query. Classes will often avoid the most critical and difficult issues. Whatever it is, I find myself taking off on this topic, where normally I let the students do the talking and I just keep it going. I will often play two sides of an issue. Sometimes I'll hear this outside voice say, "What are you doing? You're adlibbing. Stop it!" Yet afterward, the students usually tell me it was a good thing— what was needed. Then I'll know that I timed it right. If I don't hear that feedback, I know that it was the wrong time. But more often it's an inspired moment when you realize that you need to raise a difficult issue.

Still, I don't do that very often. I'll ask the students a question to get their critique going. Or sometimes they're so ready to go, they just go. At the advanced level, that's easy to do. Sometimes, though, I have to say, "I think you guys are avoiding something." I try to use my power in a positive way. Even at the beginning of the course, I tell the students, "This is *your* class. The reason we're here is to give you the chance to share your work and your ideas with each other. I'm delivering information; I'm bringing stuff in for *you*. However, you guys are sharing this experience." I try to set class up so that it's not me against them but rather a class that's much more shared, much more circular in its energy.

The boundaries can be fuzzy. A student recently sort of forgot who I was—she was joking around with me and said, "You're such an ass." Then she gasped and covered her mouth, horrified by what she'd just said." I told her, "It's okay. I am sometimes." Sometimes students call me "Dad." They say, "Dad—I mean Mark?" This reveals a level of trust. There is a familial sense to my work with students.

Still, we need boundaries. Those boundaries can be imposed. But it's much better when the respect that happens naturally defines the boundaries, when the students know I'm trying to help them and that they can trust me and that I need time and space to be an artist, a parent, a spouse, a teacher. It is important that they know I have many identities, too. This happens over time.

It's a bad day when I have to come down hard on students. But I think they realize I am critical in evaluations because it's a good time for it. It's difficult to figure out when to use a sword and when to use a carrot. Both types of power—if we're going to call it power—bring with them responsibility, responsibility that I have to the students.

I'll tell students when I'm having a bad day. I'll say to the class, "I'm having a really bad day today. If you had planned to ask for my opinion on something today and it can wait, save it for Wednesday." I don't have a poker face, and I can't pretend. I'll also let students know if it's a particularly busy or stressful time for the department. They don't need to have the details. But it helps them to know where I am and where their other teachers are. It works best to be honest.

Sister Corrita, a nun who taught in the 1960s, wrote a list of rules with one of her classes while on a fieldtrip as a guide to create a good community in the classroom. It includes rules for students: "Trust the people you're working with. Try to get everything out of them. Try to get everything out of yourself." It also includes rules for teachers: "Trust your students. Trust your colleagues." The list encourages students to go to everything all the time because it's the people who do everything all the time who end up learning and gaining opportunities. It was printed on a letterpress in funky 60s type. I picked it up at a conference and thought it could be our class document: "Students and Teachers Working Together." It tells us to be nice and try to understand things. If you work really hard, you'll get somewhere. It's not about grades. I read Sister Corrita's rules to the students on the first day, and everybody gets a copy. It ends up influencing everything we do. It creates a sense of community.

I read through my syllabus on the first day of class. The grading policy is the piece that's always a little fuzzy for me. I'm not in a discipline where we have a right answer and a wrong answer. That's the reason for the portfolio. I grade holistically. The grading policy explains, "You will be graded on your conceptual growth, your technical growth, your growth with issues of craft." You can say something is well crafted or not well crafted. But when you get to the advanced classes, a student might intentionally use craft that's traditionally considered poor. Then I can say, "You're using dirty borders to make a point, to create the sense that the piece is edged." At times, unconventional approaches are very appropriate. One of Sister Corrita's rules is, "We're breaking all of the rules all of the time and creating new rules." In my discipline that involves creative problem-solving, there's no black and white, no right and wrong.

At midterm and finals, I write students notes, giving them feedback, and at the bottom, I translate the note into a dumb little grade. I think grades are silly. I tell students that I wish we had a plus and minus system, so I give them a plus or a minus, along with the letter with their portfolios. "C" is average—the syllabus states this. An "A" is earned through outstanding effort. The students see the comments, and they see the grades. Then they either come to me and ask, "Did you really mean my work was good?" Or they say, "What can I do to improve this?" When I distribute grades, I tell them, "Don't burn down my house. No mail bombs. Email me or talk to me—something. This is the beginning of a dialogue."

At mid-semester, the students put their portfolios together. And then I ask them to write about their strengths and weaknesses. I ask them to consider how they approached their work through the semester. If that doesn't make sense to them, I prompt them: "Did you work consistently throughout the semester? Or did you do this binge and purge thing, where you were in here one week and not the next? Did you do that for a reason? Did it make sense?" I tell them I won't read their reflections; these are notes for *them*. At the end of this writing session, I'll ask them to give themselves a letter grade.

The beginning printmaking students are nervous about this. There's a point between freshman-sophomore work and junior-senior work where you have to help them make the transition from assignment-driven work to more self-designed and self-sustained work. Helping each student over the fence is the trick. Some of them think it's easy and take only a little coaching. Others are thrown into crisis. They've always been told what to do. And there are differences in discipline. The people who see themselves as painters, printmakers, sculptors, or ceramicists have an easier time. Those who see them-

Ultimately, my goal is to become obsolete. I treat them all as people who want to make art for the rest of their lives, whether it be to make a living or as a passion. I want them to learn to think independently and outside the box.

selves as functional potters don't deal with content so much; they deal with craft. They say, "What do I do?" Those with graphic design backgrounds who are accustomed to client-driven assignments also have trouble. Sometimes I have to help them to get started, making new parameters and stretching their understanding of what they can accomplish.

Ultimately, my goal is to become obsolete. I treat them all as people who want to make art for the rest of their lives, whether it be to make a living or as a passion. I want them to learn to think independently and outside the box. I tell them, "If you see me stepping away, don't get excited. I'm right there. I'm just giving you a little room." I step further and further back all the time. That's fun—to make yourself obsolete.

Outside the Classroom

As the adviser of the Student Art League, I take students on a lot of trips. I also take the printmaking students to conferences. Some of my colleagues think I'm nuts. I probably am. Things come up on these trips that have to be handled very carefully, but I'm used to doing that in the classroom. It's usually people who work in the lecture format who cannot imagine taking students on trips. But the students are adults. They can take care of themselves. I am merely facilitating an experience. I do have them sign a waiver that says I'm not going to bail them out of jail, that they're representatives of UW, and that they will keep that in mind as they make decisions. Often times, at conferences especially, the students are shopping for graduate schools. These are the core students, and they've paid to go and are taking time away from school and jobs. Sometimes I find university funds to help support the trip, but there's a certain investment that each student must make. When I took a group to a conference in Ohio, for example, we were on the road for days. We plan stops along the way; we'll visit museums. These trips help to create community. The students have a shared experience beyond the class.

Eleven students and I went to Jackson recently. They exhibited their work at the National Wildlife Art Museum in a gallery for local artists connected to the museum's café. It's an informal space, but it is a great place for the students to have their work. While we were there, we took advantage of a larger art community. For a panel discussion we brought together artists who make a living from their work and artists who work a zillion odd jobs in order to be able to live in Jackson. The panel included architects, graphic designers, and other people doing art-related work as well as painters and sculptors who work on ranches and in retail. The students gave me a list of questions they wanted to ask about art careers. And we talked about backgrounds, how these artists got to where they are. It was great because they had a variety of paths—English majors turned artists, people with BFAs, people with terminal degrees in the arts. It was nice to hear them talk about what they got from the profession as well as what they lost. The students were the instigators—they helped to organize it and they had a sense of ownership for it. Again, I was the driver. I made sure it got set up by speaking with a couple of people, and a couple of art organizations in the area. While on this trip, we also looked at a contemporary exhibition of digital interactive work at the Jackson Visual Art Association. It's good to take advantage of the resources in the state.

The fact that we crossed Wyoming to get to Jackson was important too. We weren't going to Denver. We weren't going to a city. Instead we crossed all of this rural space, we went through students' hometowns. We got to Jackson, and the students felt like the panel and the trip were pertinent to their lives and their experience.

The Student Art League used to have a space in downtown Laramie on 1st Street until the space was reclaimed by the landlord. The students took that opportunity to reevaluate. They recognized they'd put a lot of money and a lot of time into that project—they were really stretching just to monitor the space. So they decided to apply for a grant to use portable walls for exhibition space in empty stores and offices where there are no guard issues or rent. I helped them find the funding and initiate the project.

The Student Art League sees its mission as exhibiting its members' own work and practicing presentation. It's a good thing, but again we have to consider certain issues about what we exhibit and how the community views that. I have to ask myself, am I sensitive to these things without censoring? Can university students work together with communities to reach compromise on these questions?

In an effort to get to know students outside of the classroom, I encourage the students to come to my office—it's in my syllabus, but what's more important is how I present the invitation when I talk through my syllabus at the beginning of a course. I keep the syllabus short. I read through it the very first day. I start at the top with all of my contact information, and I explain to them how to find me. I say, "If you're a shy person and to talk to me would make you break down in tears, then email me first." I tell them where my office is. I can't bring myself to put a note on my office door that says, "Work in progress; please do not disturb." I understand why people do that; they can't get a lot of work done otherwise. I do have a studio at home, and I've moved much of my work there. I've sacrificed students seeing me at work on my art. Some people say, "It's so important that they see you work." Well, I have to get some work done. So I work at home. I think it is most important not to turn students away from my office. When I am interrupted in the studio, I pull out my calendar and make a time for a later date. Students can make appointments to meet with me, contact me via email, or call my office or the art office. I give students my home phone number for emergencies. Teaching studio courses places me in my office or a studio for over twenty hours of contact each week. I'm there!

We're trying to teach our students to use email. Interestingly, there's a group of students who won't go there. They're afraid. But we encourage them—the department mailings that used to go out on paper now go through email. It turns out to be a good forum for interacting with students. I've had a number of students use email as a way to protest grades. They give me their reasons, and they can think it through before they hit "Send." We start a conversation there if we don't already have the rapport. It used to bother me, because I like eye-to-eye contact, but I've decided this is a really good thing. In fact, I encourage students who are having problems in other classes to approach their professors with email. I'll even say, "Let's start drafting one here" or, "I'll read through it for you after you write it. I'll tell you how I would take it if I were the teacher." It's a nice way to start talking.

It is important to set boundaries. Yes, I'm approachable, and I'm friendly, but we all have our own time. I'm still the teacher, and there are things I don't want to know. I don't want to hear all of the complaints. Unwinding—it's really healthy, and we all do it. But in social situations when the students start to do it, I'll leave and give them room to vent without me as an audience. I'll go to the bar or a restaurant with students after they've had an exhibition. I'll bring my son Ky, and sometimes Leah, my wife, is there too, and they all know each other. We're there for a time. We support them. And then we give them time by themselves. Even in Jackson, I didn't stay in the hotel with the students; I stayed with a friend. It empowers students to know I trust them.

In the department, we've set up a Student Art Council. The department chair meets with a group of students from across the disciplines within the department once a month. She asks them questions, and they bring issues to the table. That group is called up frequently to serve in leadership roles. They help with visiting candidates, department guests, and visiting artists and scholars. They act as hosts. The students get to meet the candidates and visitors, and these departmental guests gain a complete view of the department through the students. The council helps the department, and it builds trust. Everybody wins. It's a healthy environment with a lot of communication.

The students help to define roles by passing them on to newer students. You're dealing with generations of students passing the torch. That's what keeps the program moving. Otherwise you grind to a halt. Inertia's a terrible thing. I have a sabbatical coming up that will break the continuum in my relationships with students. That's the part of the sabbatical I'm not looking forward to. I have split my sabbatical over one calendar year rather than one academic year. I did that, in part, so I won't miss any one group.

Fostering All Voices

In some courses issues of equality come up in the content. In the arts and humanities we are often discussing issues where gender and race and equality are at the heart of the subject matter. In this way, Sally Steadman's courses in engineering are very different. Equality might not come up in any explicit way in an engineering class, but the issues are still there in the classroom. Students are people. They all have issues they bring to class. These concerns don't need to come up in class, but nonetheless it needs to be a safe place to learn. If somebody has prejudices, they don't need to be on the table in the classroom; they can vent those someplace else. Hopefully, in university classrooms, we strive for an understanding that overcomes those prejudices, whatever the discipline.

Art communities tend to be small. You have to behave yourself. You have to get along with lots of other people. Also, in certain areas of printmaking, you literally need each other physically: "I need to move that stone from there to here." Sculptors have to ask each other for help too. It's interesting that members of some disciplines tend to be loan wolves. Painters, for example. They close their doors; they paint. They don't have to share recipes or share technology. In ceramics, sculpture, and printmaking, nobody's too proprietary about their processes. I encourage this kind of sharing among the students. In a really good advanced class, they'll teach each other. We have in-class critiques about every two weeks. This is when the work stops and we start to analyze. I might say to one student, "You need to look at this artist. When you leave class, go to the library." We'll look at the students' work in historical terms; we'll share articles that feed into what they're doing. Right now in one of my classes there are a lot of people working on objects that are metaphors for their lives—still-lifes that are not really still-lifes. One person has created images of broken leaves; another is dealing with blocks. It just so happens that they have a similar theme—that's not unusual. So we'll read related articles, looking at artists who have explored that theme in the past, such as Walter Benjamin's "Art in the Age of Mechanical Reproduction." These discussions lead back to their work. We'll look at what's working technically, what's working conceptually. They have to handle each other very carefully. That's not just an image up there; that's an image someone has created out of some connection to their own lives and experience. The students are learning how to give a respectful critique and how to take criticism. My job is to mediate.

We have an interesting gender thing going on right now. Just last night one of the students, a guy, said, "If you let those women get the upper hand, they'll walk all over you for the rest of your life." I asked him, "Isn't that true in any relationship where you have boundaries for what's acceptable and what's not? Is it so much about gender? Don't you find this to be true with your male friends?" Rather than trying to reshape him, I asked him to look at issues of power and interaction. He said, "I guess you're right." This story makes the student look like a hideous guy. But it's the way he's learned to talk about these issues. It's the way guys talk about these issues all of the time; it's a competitive way of interacting.

Difficult situations grow out of content and imagery, too. This year a male student made an image of a nude woman that some of the other students found offensive. The work certainly objectified the woman depicted. It should be noted that there was no trust between the artist and the other students. He was an outlier in the class. The others had tried to include him but he was always outside. I saw them extend trust, but he didn't accept it. It was an awkward class, a very diverse group in terms of backgrounds. This student was looking at pornographic sources for reference. I said, "You know, there's a difference between pornography

and erotic art. Let's talk about that." He said, "So you want me to go
look at *Playboy?*" My response was, "I think you probably already are."
I suggested we look at other sources that might talk about sexuality in a
more positive way. I gave him artists all the way back to Hindu miniatures. "Here's how the Japanese dealt with sexuality in pillow books. This
is very erotic stuff—they're how-to books, but these are also very beautiful images." We started looking at a variety of sources and how those fit
into the cultures they came from. He wasn't very scholarly. Most often, I
felt obligated to thrust the alternatives on him. Had he wanted to learn at
that time, this would have been a great opportunity. But he was someone
who, I think, wanted to shake the class up a bit. Rather than figure out
how to handle both the craft and the content, he was dealing only with
the content he knew would distract the class. I got to the point where I
said, "Okay, let's forget about the content. We're going to talk about these
as prints—what's working technically, what's not." The student was
avoiding learning the skills he needed, and I decided to stop pushing.

I was careful at that point not to let the students talk about the content in his work. At the end of the semester one of the post-baccalaureate
students assisting me with the class said to me, "Will you let go of the
leads now?" She knew I'd been reining them in. I asked her to tell me
exactly what she had in mind. She said, "I just want him to take responsibility for his work. I think it's time. I think the beginning class can do it,
and they can do it in a good way." So at the final critique, he got the
blast of what he'd needed to hear the whole time. I invited the students
to talk about the content of the student's entire body of work. They did
it well. And he was all right; he didn't break down. They did it in a very
clear, forceful way, but it was sensitive. I was really proud of the class. It
was important for the students to voice their opinions. Part of what this
class is about is learning the language to talk about art, and they had that
by the end of the semester.

I don't want to censor the students' art. But I do want them to take
responsibility for it. To make matters more complicated, the artist was
African American in an all white class. Throughout the semester he
stated that he felt that criticism of his work stemmed from his race.
During the final critique, I suggested we change the discussion of the image that was sexist, that we make it an image that objectified race. It
made the point to the student. As a white instructor this was a potentially

difficult and dangerous thing to do. I am an adoptive parent of a Korean child. I think that has actually allowed me to put some really sensitive issues of race on the table. In this case it allowed us to use race to talk about sexism.

Actually that was a milestone in my teaching career. I had dealt with issues of race before, but there had been students with other ethnicities at the table. It wasn't one minority student facing a white teacher with a white student peer group. It was easier in the past at other institutions that had a more racially diverse student body, because the racial issues had been on the surface— all the time, every day, for years. In contrast, the students in the situation I just outlined put the issues on the table because they wanted them there.

> I want students to think about what they really want to say, no matter who they are. Creating an atmosphere of trust becomes critical.

All of the students have a voice in their own education. We don't just encourage it. We require it. We'll tell them, "You're going to be making art in a hostile environment because you live in the United States where art's not considered part of everybody's daily life." If the students continue to make art after they graduate, especially outside of the applied-arts fields, I think we've succeeded in creating confident, happy students who are able to continue finding the resources they need. But I think there's something separate from having them find their voices as students and then as young professionals. It's also important to help them find their voices as artists: What do you want to say? How do you want to say it? That's what the advanced classes are all about. In some ways differentiating that this student is gay or lesbian or that another student is Hispanic or Anglo becomes secondary. It doesn't really matter. I care, but that's not something that changes the dialogue. I want students to think about what they really want to say, no matter who they are. Creating an atmosphere of trust becomes critical.

Currently I have a student who is lesbian, and she feels very comfortable in the class. She feels that trust is there and that she can do what she needs to. She also has a support group beyond this class that deals with gay and lesbian issues. I think the students from racial minorities also have places they can go to have that dialogue. Oddly enough, the students who are dealing—maybe for the first time—with the notion that the whole world isn't white are the ones who don't have a place where they can talk about it. They don't feel like they can talk about it— somehow it's really dangerous. The students—especially the male students—who are dealing with discussions about gender in the classroom also don't have a place where they can talk about the experience outside of the guy-guy sports bar environment. That's *a* place, but it's maybe not the most positive place. It's not the same thing as having the true, meaningful dialogue that happens in these other supportive environments. We have women's studies classes, but we don't have many classes that deal with gender study broadly. A few writers have written about what it means to be white and male at the beginning of the twenty-first century. We have writers who have written about what it means to be white, male, and gay. But there aren't many white male heterosexuals who are writing about gender and race issues. They could ask, "What do I have to offer? Am I just the bad guy? How can I be part of a celebration of diversity, even if I'm part of the majority?" Defining of self is what these students are doing: Who am I? What am I? What does it mean to be alive and human?

The white male students who have wonderful things to say feel like they shouldn't say them because it's too dangerous. It's funny—it's really not dangerous at all. The students who really do have identity issues that put them at risk and put themselves on the line say, "What do *you* have to be afraid of?" But the white students feel they're almost insulting minority students to complain or be critical about anything. It's hypersensitivity. Can we get rid of all of that? We need to figure out how to make everybody feel safe, even the people who have every reason to feel safe but for some reason don't. I have one student who, on the edge of tears, told me, "I'm always just a dumb white guy asking questions." The women are a little hard on him. Granted, there are times when he phrases things in a way that sets him up for disaster. But he truly cares. That's a hard situation to navigate.

If I can help someone who's not from a racial majority or someone who's putting their homosexuality out in the world, how can I help the students who *should* be really comfortable truly feel comfortable as well? Especially when we have more sensitive discussions going on. Right now I have a student who's coming from a religiously conservative background. His father's a minister. He's actually really open and comfortable with everyone in the classroom, including an openly lesbian student and two women who are very involved in women's studies classes and making all sorts of discoveries there. All of them get along. Something's working. But two white guys still feel hesitant. When others are defining themselves through difference, it's hard for these two to define *themselves* at all.

Difference is only one way to define self. It's really wonderful that for the student who is out and lesbian, her work's not about that at all. It's a part of her daily life; it's a part of what she talks about. She might mention her partner, but that's not what the work's about. Some of the other students wonder what they have to offer that's unique and important. I say, "Well, your ranch background is probably important. I see you talking about that experience in this work." When I take students to conferences, they tend to think, "I'm from Wyoming; I have nothing to offer." I tell them, "No, you're an exotic flower. It's just that you're in a hothouse full of exotic flowers right now." One student returning from a domestic exchange asked me, "Do you know that in Chicago people buy their Christmas trees at Christmas tree stands? I just didn't understand why they didn't go to the mountains and get their own tree." These students go someplace else and realize what a strange and wonderful *daily* life they have. For students to realize that what they have is different, they have to leave. That's helping students find their voice.

We need to work on social equality in the university environment. People who are teaching are often from privileged backgrounds. As a group we lack an awareness and experience with the background of many of our students. There's often an economic difference between those who can go to university and those who do not attend a university. We're slowly bridging that. Class isn't obvious. We don't see it, and we often cannot discern it in speech. We tend to believe that we live in a relatively classless society. That's not quite true. We do a pretty good job addressing issues of class at the University of Wyoming because we have so many first-generation university students. We have to structure our curriculum and programming for first-generation students. We have the Office of Student Educational Opportunity. I can say to students, "There is a program for first-generation students that will let you know about scholarships you might not otherwise find."

I have a lot of these students, and I think they feel especially comfortable with me after they learn I have the same background. I tell them the first day that I was the first person in my family to go to college. I say, "I'm going to tell you just a little bit about me—I'll try not to bore you to tears. I'm going to give you a brief biography so that you can listen through me. When you're rolling your eyes at me, at least you'll know where I'm coming from." So I tell them where I grew up and where I did my university education. And I tell them I'm from a blue-collar background, one generation off the farm. These things color my teaching, help me to relate to some of the students better.

Socioeconomic issues come up all of the time. First-generation students limit themselves in terms of what they can do. They'll say, for example, "I *have* to work in the applied arts." They lack self-confidence. They're worried about what their parents will think. I experienced this. I remember going to my adviser and saying, "I don't think I want to be an illustrator. I really like to draw. But how will I eat? What will I do?" She talked me through it. I use part of that conversation with my students. I ask them, "What's the most difficult and least desirable job you can imagine?" Mine was being a garbage collector. Then I point out that with that job they would eat; they would live. I also note that with that job they could continue making art. Or we'll talk about what skills they have, how they might use those skills that are outside of art in order to support themselves. These conversations help them to figure out how their careers might work.

Communication with the family helps. Students will show their parents portfolios of their work, tell them what it is they do. Often, the parents will say, "Great. We are so glad you're following your heart. Do this. If you need to work a blue-collar job, that's fine; just don't feel like it's been imposed on you."

Often, first-generation students lack knowledge about what's available to them. It becomes important for me to say, "Did you know these resources were available to you?" Fostering all voices in the classroom ultimately comes back to a trust between the student and the instructor and asking questions that the student might not even know are necessary to foster their growth.

Role Models

From high school on, I had role models—working artists who taught. One of my high school teachers did this, and I worked as his assistant. When I went to a university, I thought I would be a medical illustrator but then decided I didn't really want to do that—I drew in a cadaver lab and realized I wanted to make drawings, not illustrations. I had an instructor I trusted. She pushed me and supported me as I made the difficult decision to leave the applied arts and pursue the fine arts. Another instructor was hideous. He "honied" and "deared" every woman in the class. He was a bad teacher. But he was a terrific artist and wonderful person to work for. I learned so much by working as a studio assistant in his home studio. I gained a better understanding about the creative process. At the same time, someone who was much closer as an adviser—a woman—taught in ways that have influenced me as an artist-teacher.

In graduate school I learned what not to do. I had instructors who weren't there, who really didn't know us. Lack of sensitivity, scapegoating, pitting students against one another, creating power struggles in the classrooms: these were all problems. It was the military approach to education—we're going to tear you down to build you up. And we'll create competition so that the best rise to the top. It was a particular method. I functioned in it. It made me stronger, more sure of what I didn't want to do. But I think I probably could have learned better in another way. A lot of how I choose to model my life and teaching I've learned from my past teachers—the good ones and the bad ones. And oddly, Sister Corrita and that scrap of paper with her rules have acted as a catalyst or a manifesto of my philosophy. She voiced much of what I seem to believe simply and directly.

Maybe some students learn well in competitive environments. But I think students, especially those who are from rural backgrounds, learn better when they are comfortable and at ease with the instructors, when there is mutual trust, and when the instructor can provide individual attention. They're being challenged, but we put trust into place first. When they look for graduate programs, I have to be honest. I'll tell them what I know about a given program and say, "I don't know whether that would suit you. I want you to consider how you learn best. I want you to know that this program is different from your undergraduate experience." Sometimes students don't know there are other approaches.

Epilogue

At the University of Wyoming in the visual arts, we are united in our desire to present ourselves to students and the community as artists who teach. It's important that the students see us outside the teacher role. We're actively making art and we are whole people. There's this myth that students have: if you're a real artist, you're in your studio twenty-four hours a day, seven days a week. My response to that is—Have a life! Art comes from life; it's part of life. It's woven into life. Art made in a vacuum cannot be sustained for long. That's one of the pitfalls of graduate school. Students will have a certain amount of source material but they don't have a life. Suddenly they run out of material, and their lives implode. I try to model for students that teaching means I'm giving information to you and getting information from you. This is a place of exchange. I want them to see that I'm learning from them sometimes. Students will ask me how to do something that I don't know how to do. So I say, "Let's open the book and work on this together. I'll make a few phone calls to colleagues who are doing this. Let's experiment." Ignorance, especially in fields that shift continuously, is the impetus for learning. I can model that—easily.

The tools change, but what we're talking about is making art. We might use printmaking as the excuse, or drawing, or the computer, or mud and sticks. But it's about ideas and the marriage of materials and ideas. We use the word *play* a lot in the art department. I know colleagues say, "You're over there playing?" This just means you are not approaching the project with a specific outcome in mind. There is a goal, but no predetermined outcome. The idea of play is important to the formation of a creative community of students. When a sense of play is healthy, they forget they're students and behave like artists. This is when the real learning begins.

Encountering Diverse Worlds

Julie Sellers
Modern and Classical Languages

I am an assistant lecturer of Spanish at the University of Wyoming. I'm originally from Kansas, and I attended Kansas State University where I earned bachelor's degrees in Spanish and French and a master's in Spanish. I have also completed a master's in international studies here at UW. Currently, I am enrolled in UW's adult learning and technology doctoral program. My research interests are quite varied. I am very pleased that my book about Dominican identity and the Dominican national dance, the merengue, will be published next year. I'm also investigating better methods to teach foreign language, especially composition.

Julie was a wonderful teacher, helping make my first semester at UW a great one. She always welcomed questions and never made any of us feel stupid for not understanding a concept right away. She had an awesome method of teaching that helped me learn Spanish to the best of my ability. No one in the class was ever singled out for any reason, and she never made inappropriate comments.

—Student nominator

I thought participating in this project would benefit me personally and benefit my teaching. I want to learn more about inequality in the classroom and become more aware of things I do and the ways I could improve. By listening and talking with the other participants, I hope to better understand what it is I do in the classroom to warm up the chill and to learn good ideas from them that I might be able to apply to my own field.

The Context of Work with Students

I teach almost exclusively third-year Spanish composition and conversation courses. In the fall, I also co-teach a seminar on identity in the Americas with a colleague in political science. My first priority is teaching; that's my job. Sometimes other things have to take second place. I fit other things around teaching because I'm not just earning a paycheck. I'm responsible to sixty-some students each semester. If they don't learn or if there's a problem and they feel uncomfortable, that's partially my fault.

Teaching to the Whole Person

It's important to try to know your students and not just their names. I know some teachers don't even know their students' names, so that's a first step. I hand out an information sheet the first day of class that asks questions about their major, whether they've studied abroad, any interests they have, and what they think about composition, talking, or speaking in public. One item says, "Tell me anything you want to or that you're concerned about." This is important because many students are inhibited to speak; many feel they can't write a decent sentence. They'll tell me that. If anyone has taken the time to write that down, then I respond, so we make a connection right off. That's the first step, getting to know them, their backgrounds and their concerns.

The second step is making reference to those things that are important to students. It makes them feel a part of the class, and they're pleased that I remember their interests and what makes them unique. They like to know that I care when they're there and when they're not. Or that I care they've been sick. The next day, I say, "Are you better?" They feel good knowing that I've missed their presence, that it is important in the class. A lot of the activities are individualized. We do journal writing in the composition course, and they write about whatever they want in Spanish. I don't grade it for grammar; I simply read it and write back to them. Some have asked me for advice. Some have told me about their Valentine's Day, or when they met their first love. I write back—whatever comes to mind—responding to what they wrote and answering any questions they might have.

In the conversation class, we don't write as much, but I have them bring in pictures of their family sometimes, asking them to tell a story about that person. I think they begin to feel that even though there are criteria—it's an assignment—class is still open and they can make it fit themselves. When I respond, they know I'm listening to them. I try to encourage them to see me and let me know any needs or goals they have, even those that don't have anything to do with the classroom. That's important, too, because they know I want to help them beyond this specific class.

The Teacher-Student Relationship: Negotiating Power

I never really thought of the difference between teachers and students as one of power. I'd always thought that someone has to be in charge, more of an *authority* figure, I suppose, who deserves respect. The degrees on the wall give me the authority at this point in the experience. I try to see myself as a guide. I can't open up their heads and pour the information in. I can't make them want to learn if they're strapped for time. So I try to provide them with the tools they need to learn.

Inside the Classroom

My syllabus is always very specific from the first day; students know what we're going to do each day. They know the pages to look at, and they can ask questions. At first they think we're going to go over those page numbers word for word. But I explain that what I want them to do is look at the information on those pages and be familiar with it. Then we'll apply it in other activities. Their job is to look over information, and then I'll guide them all on how to use it. I sometimes tell them I'm like their tour guide and their book and their notes are like the map. If they don't open up the map, they're going to get lost. Likewise, the tour guide is a leader, a guide—not a magician who magically and instantly can make them learn and know what we've covered.

I see the classroom as collaborative. Certainly, there is a difference between them and me. Somebody has to determine the grade in the end. But I think that you can make it a comfortable setting by emphasizing that you're there to help them, that you're collaborating, and that you want each individual to succeed. I try to emphasize that I set rules so that everybody has equal footing, so that there is some semblance of standards. Then I just expect students to follow the rules. For the most part they do.

I have developed accompanying course packets for my classes. The conversation textbook, for example, doesn't deal directly with grammar, and they need to review it. I always try to make the activities in these packets relevant to the students. That makes a difference. I've had people say, "This must take a lot of time." I know students appreciate it.

In the conversation class, I have started writing each quiz as one episode of a soap opera. They know this takes a lot of time, too. It's a story—there are characters, there's a plot. Every episode ends with a cliff-hanger. And the final exam resolves everything. The quizzes ask the students to fill in the blank with vocabulary or a grammar form, or to respond to the situation in the plot. Someone outside of the class helps me record a conversation between the two main characters, and students have to listen and answer related questions. Students do better with this test format because they enjoy it more and they're more involved. The students get into the story and begin to talk about the characters. Last semester one student said, "I'm so glad Rafael and Andrea got together in the end." She was worried that they wouldn't resolve their problems and would end up separated. The grades were higher using this format. If students feel comfortable and if—heaven forbid—they enjoy the work, they are more engaged in the quiz items and do better.

The students don't take a final exam in my composition courses; rather, they write a final three-to-five page research paper. They have the opportunity to do as much of a first draft as they can, on which I make some corrections and offer suggestions. Then, they work on a final draft. The class works through the entire process of writing a paper—choosing a topic, finding sources, discussing how to write a thesis statement, talking about how to do a correct bibliography and citations. I look at their specific questions, and they also get a lot of practice in self-editing. The topic is open, and I ask them to choose something that really interests them. I tell them they're not in a situation where they have to address a given topic; this can be about whatever they want because the main goal is to enjoy researching and learning about the topic, and then communicating that information about it. They get much more involved this way. They include pictures, they make entire folders. Many turn it into something far more than a research paper. I ask them to decide what interests them and what their opinions are on the subjects they choose. I give them specific objectives with regard to grammar, style, and the components of a good paper. But beyond that, it's open. This process makes them feel like they're taking part in and determining their own education. The work truly represents them.

There have certainly been instances when I should have handled power in the classroom differently. In one course, a young man who knew quite a bit of Spanish tried to prove that he knew everything there was to know—the whole semester long. He had a group of friends in class, and they would sit and snicker in the back. Other students told me they couldn't hear, they didn't appreciate it. The student's behavior was really interfering. I wish I would have asked him to come to my office or explained to him outside of the classroom that what he was doing wasn't acceptable instead of trying to shift the conversation or mood in class each time he acted up. In one of the adult education classes I have taken, we talked about problem students. It seems like there is no one way to handle them. I always worry about being too authoritative, but I probably should have been more authoritative in this case for the sake of everybody else. Next time—if this happens again—I'd like to try a technique I learned in the adult education class: I'll ask the student to *write* his or her complaint. I would say, "Write down exactly what your problem is with me, because you clearly have one." Generally students can't put the problem into words, or if they do, they're going to realize that they can't really specify the problem as solely external to them.

Outside the Classroom

I tell every class that I feel like the Maytag repairman in my office. I really wish they'd come and visit with me. I encourage them over and over to come see me or send an email if they have questions on anything we're doing or if we haven't covered a topic to the extent they'd like. Before quizzes, I remind them they can always call or email me. I know that my students have a lot of pressures. I would like for them to be studying all along, but they might not be able to until a couple nights before. I would hate for them to be studying the night before a quiz or to be working on a paper right before it's due and think, oh my gosh, I don't understand this and the quiz is tomorrow or the paper's due tomorrow, and I can't ask her.

I tell them to set up an appointment if my office hours don't work. There's a line on my syllabus that says, "*Please* make an appointment. I'm always willing to make appointments whenever they're more convenient for you." Some students will just drop by, too. Every semester, I find that some students will take the initiative. They find out that it's not that bad, that I don't bite. They come to talk about class and many come to talk about study abroad. For example, one stopped in recently to ask if I knew anything about Puebla, México; she wanted to go there. I had been to Puebla—I hadn't studied there, but I had been there. I got down my photo album, and we chatted about it. Sometimes if students are in the building, they'll stop in and say, "Are you ready to go to class?" And we'll walk over together. They start to feel really comfortable, and I'm always very glad about that.

My office is adorned with visual aids. Students like that—it makes a personal connection. Here's someone who's been there; here's someone who says something that reminds me of my experience abroad. These things help make the language seem more concrete and real, and they also help students get to know me through these objects. I bring in pictures of my family when we tell family anecdotes in class, or I include pictures from my trips abroad and tell personal anecdotes. That helps them see that I'm a real person, and I think it also shows my enthusiasm for Spanish and Hispanic cultures.

People often come to visit with me about their level of fluency. In the third year, you have a wide spectrum: people who started here at UW and had so much interest they continued; people who had some Spanish in high school and then skipped a little further ahead; some who studied abroad; some who learned abroad as missionaries. There's always a group that hasn't had the opportunity to study abroad yet, and they're afraid. Some of the biggest, strongest guys on this campus come in and inform me they're afraid to talk or they're afraid of so and so who sits by them. Some of the individuals who have lived abroad aren't speaking perfectly, but they have an ease with speaking because they have *had* to speak. To other students, it sounds like they're perfect. So I always appreciate it when someone comes in and tells me they're afraid. I can usually tap in to several intimidated students. The person in my office has friends in the class. And that person will repeat back to the friends what I've told him: "They're not perfect. They're in here because they don't know everything." I encourage the student to speak. I say, "If anyone laughs at you, I will take care of it."

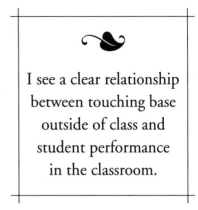

I see a clear relationship between touching base outside of class and student performance in the classroom.

I think that every time someone has come in to talk with me about feeling intimidated, they end up feeling comfortable enough to start speaking even a little more in class. Then the other students see that, and they follow suit. I see a clear relationship between touching base outside of class and student performance in the classroom.

At UW, we've been able to send students abroad through ISEP—the International Student Exchange Program—for a long time. It's a gamble, though: students might want to go to Spain, but only so many people can go to Spain, so they have to list other choices. We also have a trip through our department—three weeks in Latin America. Individuals have gone to Costa Rica and Ecuador, and this summer they're going to Bolivia. That's such a short amount of time, but it works well. It fits pre-session—a lot of students will go on the three-week trip, then come back and take my conversation class in June, so they get three weeks there, three weeks here.

Our newest program is an exchange with various institutes in Spain. Students can go for a semester, for a year, or during the summer, and they have a variety of classes from which to choose, from language, culture and literature courses to courses with Spaniards in many areas. There are specialized programs in some cities for engineering and business courses, too. It's a good price. They pay UW tuition, and we have an arrangement with the program so it's a little bit less expensive than it might be otherwise. Students who have gone cannot say enough good things about their experience. Any time students mention study-abroad programs, I tell them to go because it's a great opportunity and a wonderful experience. We should have more of this type of program—in Latin America and South America.

Social differences influence who can study abroad. And that's important for learning the language and feeling confident. Some students just don't have the money, and no matter what they do, they're not going to get it. They can't take out a loan, because maybe they're already in debt. That's one thing I'd like to look into—how can we get these students abroad? How does it influence their performance, their achievement? I continue to look for ways for *all* students—including those who couldn't afford it on their own—to have a chance to travel.

Students really learn the language and gain confidence when they study abroad. When students return, they can speak what people really speak—more of the street language, the slang, with a more authentic rhythm and accent. And they're motivated to speak, to practice. They've been using Spanish everyday, and they miss it. They look for opportunities outside the classroom to use the language. Studies abroad are an effective and life-changing way to learn.

Fostering All Voices

It's always helpful to have a small class. Unfortunately, we can't. My smallest is eighteen. Among foreign language educators, a maximum of twelve to fifteen learners is considered an optimal class size. So eighteen isn't bad. But my conversation class is twenty-five, and that's really difficult. The class always has to be in a larger room, which makes it seem like it's even bigger. In all my classes, I often divide people into pairs and other sizes of groups. I count them off, making sure that I mix them up so that they work with different classmates. This method serves the double purpose of giving them smaller groups so all can participate and of allowing them to get to know more about each other. For me, one of the most rewarding aspects of teaching is watching friendships develop among students who didn't even know each other before the class began.

Generally, students aren't afraid to talk in a group of three or four— that gives them the opportunity to participate. I go around and listen, and I make comments about what they're saying, so they know I'm listening, even though it's not in a whole-group setting. That's one way to give everyone a chance.

Another approach is to watch students' eyes. I'll see when someone has an idea but doesn't express it. If you say, "What do you think?"—not *"Answer!"* but "What do you think?"—they will usually join in. Sometimes to break the ice, maybe when we're doing grammar exercises, we'll go around the room so everybody has to read. That levels the playing field. I remind them that we all make mistakes when we speak, even in English. They always seem to feel pretty comfortable with the way I correct them. I don't say, "You're wrong" but "Well, let's think about it." Or I'll reapply the rule at hand. It takes a conscious effort to correct in such a way that students don't feel chastised or embarrassed. When I correct with these techniques, the students seem to understand that making mistakes is part of the learning process and they don't seem to mind if they do make mistakes and are corrected.

I try to encourage all voices in individualized assignments, such as the journals used in my composition classes. This type of assignment gives them a voice in case they're not the type to speak out in class, and it allows them one-on-one contact with me, the instructor. They can often communicate more freely with me that way.

Including different types of activities within the class is another technique to foster all student voices. Some learners excel in writing, so I assign writing in groups to give them the chance to show what they're really good at. Also, we do a lot of skits in the conversation class. Skits allow everyone to talk—of course they all have to. They will match their part in the scene to how comfortable they feel—a quiet role or a more outgoing role. Sometimes they might play a role totally different from their personality. Since it's acting, they feel comfortable experimenting. These are all ways to give students a voice. Sometimes giving everyone a chance involves taking some students aside and asking them to talk a bit less because you can tell they're intimidating those who would say something otherwise.

Participation is part of the grade in my classes. Part of the criteria I give out on the first day includes, "If you speak out all of the time, your grade will drop. That's not part of being a good conversationalist." I've gone so far as to make up names and give descriptions—always with a former student and experience in mind—of what I think makes a below-average and average participator, what I think makes a good or superior participator, and what I think makes an overachiever—someone who needs to be more quiet. It works pretty well to give them concrete examples this way. I go through this criteria at the beginning of the semester, and I haven't had too many problems. I let students know from the first day what I expect. And I give about five participation grades throughout the semester—five or six—so they have plenty of time to redeem themselves if they don't get off on the right foot.

A lot of the students like to email me in Spanish. I think it's fun for them; it's like experimenting with the language in a whole new realm. They love it. A lot of them will write and say, "Here's a question I have." And then I respond. They seem almost honored that I respond to them in Spanish. Many of them comment, "Yeah, I've had so and so mark all over my paper, but I never understood why, and when I went to ask them, they talked to me in English." So I think they appreciate that I use Spanish with them when they write me in Spanish. Maybe they feel more comfortable with these conversations when they're in email because they can reread them and revise. It's an easy way to get in touch with me. If they have mono or the flu and can't bring in an assignment, they can attach it to an email message so that we can keep up to date. A couple of my students had very bad illnesses in the family this year and they had to leave immediately. I was able to send them updates via email of exactly what we did in class. I could keep their email address on my computer until they returned. I could keep them up to date, and I didn't have to remember later the dates they were gone and what we did on those days. I find email very useful.

With regard to equality in the classroom, one thing that interests me is representation in our textbooks. Sometimes they're male dominated—that's who the characters are in the textbooks, and when the textbook authors write about the great authors and artists, it's men who mostly come up. Sometimes the textbooks try to include women, but they'll go to extremes using examples that aren't realistic. One textbook had a chapter about a divorced woman, but it didn't seem like she was real—she seemed very forced. To make it worse, that book used cartoons rather than real photos, so it seemed even more false. If authors want to include a divorced woman, they should interview a woman in Spain or Chile and take a picture of her and let *her* speak and tell her own story.

We get a lot of unrealistic cultural representation in the textbooks. These are the ideas students have of the culture before they go to visit

Spanish-speaking countries. I try to use representations outside of the textbooks, like programs I tape off television, my own news clippings, magazines, and menus, or even the cheesy *Hola* magazine from Walmart that's like the *National Enquirer*. I look for anything that shows what the people in a given country are doing, what the current fads or concerns are, who and what's cool and popular. I get online and look at Yahoo en Español for news, or Univisión.com to find current events to discuss with the students.

I also try to work with the students on questions of race as it affects identity in individual Latin American cultures. Sometimes these issues can be difficult for students to discuss, especially in a foreign language. They don't quite know what to think—they came to learn the subjunctive, not to talk about race, class, and gender issues.

I went to the Dominican Republic in 1993 and worked on a community-service project. Then later, working on my master's degree in international studies, I researched issues of identity in the Dominican Republic. Specifically, I researched

We get a lot of unrealistic cultural representation in the textbooks. These are the ideas students have of the culture before they go to visit Spanish-speaking countries.

their national dance, the merengue, because Dominicans would swear it was in their blood and that it was *them*. It was such a strong pillar of their identity. I began to look at the merengue in terms of race, gender, and politics. In fact, the dance was used as a device of political control for thirty years from 1930–1961 under the dictator Raphael Trujillo, who appropriated it for nation-building and identity consolidation purposes. At social functions, if people didn't play his favorite merengue, which was about his hometown, they could disappear. The merengue is a mix of three ethnicities, the indigenous, the European, and the African. Yet, despite the merengue's highly Afro-Caribbean sounds, it's claimed to be a primarily Hispanic creation, meaning its European roots are emphasized. Likewise, Dominican identity has long been claimed to be primarily

Hispanic, secondarily indigenous, with the African element almost completely downplayed. Dominicans associate blackness with Haiti, and due to a conflictive history with their neighboring country, they hold a lot of animosity towards that race. Furthermore, race is also determined in the Dominican Republic by social class. For example, a darker complexioned Dominican of the small upper class would be considered white. We have to ask ourselves, what does it mean to be black or white or indigenous in the Dominican Republic and elsewhere? The definitions of these categories aren't the same there as they are here or in Peru or elsewhere. This example shows us that race is constructed according to what people want race to do for them.

I bring this idea into the classroom. The students and I talk about it. I show a good video about the Dominican Republic, so they can see what the place and the people who live there look like. A lot of these students don't have any idea that there were that many Africans brought as slaves to the Caribbean. They associate slavery with the south in their own country. They begin to see the wide varieties among people—the ways they live, the ways they look. It makes students, especially those who haven't traveled much, see that *white* is not white as Americans see it everywhere. The questions of identity make students rethink their own preconceived ideas, their own history, their own prejudices.

Recently I've begun co-teaching a seminar in political science entitled Identity in the Americas, and we study the Dominican Republic, among other countries, in this course, too. During each class session, my colleague and I try to bring the discussion full circle by applying topics and theories studied to the students themselves as citizens of Wyoming or other states, the United States, and the Americas. At the end of the semester, students write an extensive paper about their own identity and discuss how they believe they came to be who they are, citing texts, topics, and theories used in the course.

Before I first went abroad, I had some very mistaken views about Latin American realities. You have a textbook that talks about tacos and piñatas and the Day of the Dead, but that's Mexican culture. The textbook doesn't show you the Dominican Republic, for example. When I went as an undergraduate, I didn't know what the people there would look like or what their reality was. When the other students and I got there, we thought that Dominicans didn't look anything like the pictures we'd usually seen in our textbooks. We thought that in the United States, Dominicans would be categorized as black. But they considered themselves white. Why hadn't our teachers taught us more about cultural differences, that those who would be called "black" in one place might be called "white" in another? I think issues of race in the countries whose language we're studying are an essential part of understanding that culture and that language.

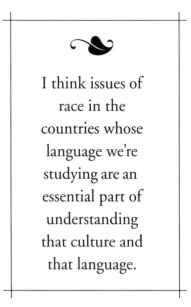

I think issues of race in the countries whose language we're studying are an essential part of understanding that culture and that language.

My friends and I had a lot of misinformation about the Dominican Republic in general. For example, we were told to take a lot of pencils because the street children beg for pencils. When we got there, we realized they were begging for *pesos*, not pencils. The Dominican Republic is a poorer country, and students should have an idea of that reality.

The Spanish-speaking world is extensive, and I don't know everything. I'll ask students who have studied abroad to speak up when we talk about other countries. I also point out that the United States has its own Hispanic culture. I offer a PowerPoint presentation on my website about Hispanic Americans, and I ask my classes to read it for class discussion. It's important for them to know that textbooks don't tell the whole story. Our language teaching is too focused on grammar and literature. We need better books and more real-life situations.

Role Models

I have one role model I always keep in mind, my major professor at Kansas State. She was difficult, that is, challenging, but she was fair. She emphasized memorizing dates and facts and lists, so her Spanish literature classes weren't easy. She tended to apply the remotest things you could imagine on a test, so she made us think. But she was definitely fair. I keep her in mind because I want to be fair to everybody. I have some instructors in mind that I don't think were fair, that I think had attitudes, that I think only cared about research and didn't care about teaching their students. Some teachers, it seemed, tried to make them fail. Those people I keep in mind so I don't act like them.

I was in a PhD program in Spanish literature for one year. There were four new PhD students, but the program involved a total of forty-some in the master's and PhD programs. It was a large program, well known, one of the best at that time. The program was competitive among the students, and it was competitive among the professors. There was one professor who gave his favorites As; those who weren't his favorites got lower grades. I have a friend who had a 4.0 from high school on, and she got a C in that class.

I had one professor who decided that because I was working ahead on my paper she could keep changing her mind about what she wanted in it, and I could keep adding to it. The criteria for it kept changing; they fluctuated constantly. It was as if she didn't think anyone should be able to start and therefore finish early. She didn't care about my goals or interests in the topic, which interested me at first but not by the end. Instead of cultivating my interests and my passion for literature, she squelched it. She didn't want to support me through the process. That paper ended up being sixty-five pages long—from an original requirement of twenty to twenty-five pages.

As far as the students were concerned, they adopted the same competitive attitudes. If there were books in the library required for a course that couldn't be checked out, some students would hide them so only they knew where they were. The rest of us couldn't find them.

One young woman from Spain, who had never before been out of the country, had come to do a master's. She started suffering panic attacks from all of the stress, and the professors honestly did not care. A few of us helped her get to the doctor, and finally she wanted to talk to a counselor on campus, so my friend went with her to help her answer the counselor's questions. The receptionist asked what department they were from. They told her, and she said, "Oh, we see your people over here all the time." It seemed to me that the department ought to want to correct that problem, but that wasn't the case.

From my experience with the sixty-five page paper, I've learned how important it is to give clear, consistent criteria. For the composition class,

I give a specific list of objectives for every paper, including grammar, vocabulary, and composition techniques, and I grade only what we have covered. The way I was taught—the way much foreign language composition is taught—is that in the third year, you should know these things. The idea is that you'll be reviewing all semester but should know everything from the beginning. Well, some students have not been taught the harder grammar or not taught effectively. For some of them, it's been too long. Some have learned primarily orally, such as heritage learners or some returned missionaries, so asking them to write is asking a lot. Still others just don't have a solid background in composition in their own language. My strategy evens the playing field. If we've only reviewed present tense, then that's the only thing I'll take points off for. I'll mark the other things, so they're aware they need work on those elements of grammar when we do cover them, but I will not deduct points for those issues. The learning and student satisfaction have certainly improved. Even elements that would have given them trouble had I been grading them aren't causing them as many problems. The students are not second-guessing themselves as much. They know what they're responsible for, and they focus on that. The other falls into place. For this reason, I also give very specific objectives in the conversation class before quizzes. I tell them exactly what will be covered and exactly what I'll take points off for, so they know going in what the conditions and criteria are.

Epilogue

Creating a sense of comfort and community in any classroom is very important. In foreign language learning, it's essential—or at least it should be—because there is an added element of risk in speaking another language. Learners need to feel supported, not just by the instructor but by their classmates. Students are clearly more motivated to learn when they feel respected and appreciated. I want them to know I have an interest in them as individuals, not just as students—to know that I notice when they're absent, or when they seem to have something on their minds that's making it hard to pay attention or participate or study on a given day. Teaching students isn't just about getting them from point A at the beginning of the semester to point B at the end—it's far more complicated than that. It's about giving them the tools to learn, guiding them in the process, exposing them to situations and activities that help them grow, and most importantly providing them with a positive learning experience so they'll want to keep on learning once the class is over.

Just as learning is a collaborative effort, creating that type of classroom atmosphere is collaborative as well. I have to set the precedence for others to follow, or students will just shut themselves up inside a shell or maybe treat their classmates with disinterest or disrespect. If I'm open and clearly interested in knowing my students' names *and* my students, and if I treat everyone with respect, then that sets the tone. True, there are those who won't follow my lead, and they present a different challenge each time.

I guess what it all boils down to, what's really the essence of warming up the chill in the classroom, is taking a genuine interest in the learners—their names, their interests, their individual goals, and their challenges—taking a genuine interest in them as fellow human beings. Add to that a good dose of compassion, and I think well over half the battle is won.

Collaborating to Learn

Sally Steadman
Engineering

I graduated over thirty years ago from the University of Wyoming with a degree in architectural engineering. At that time, teaching was probably the last career that I was considering. However, by chance I ended up teaching at a community college and found my life's work. I subsequently earned a master's degree in mathematics and a PhD in mechanical engineering to be able to teach in higher education. Along the way, I discovered that I really enjoy working with computer applica-

Being a female minority student in the College of Engineering is rare at the University of Wyoming. Ms. Steadman has not only been my major support but a mentor to me in my studies. At a point in my college career I felt like I was not headed in the right direction, and it was Sally whom I talked with to lead me in a more confident direction. Her effective teaching skills display her ability to help each student to succeed no matter what background they might come from.

—Student nominator

tions. Before coming to UW, I worked in several national labs, including what is now the National Renewable Energy Laboratory, doing consulting and training for computer users. I also served as assistant computing center director at the Colorado School of Mines. I've been at UW since 1984. I was initially hired to facilitate computing in the curriculum. I continued to take classes toward my PhD and completed it in 1994. My dissertation is in the area of expert systems, a subset of artificial intelligence.

I am particularly interested in working with women and minorities—underrepresented populations—in engineering. I've also been involved in recruiting these populations to engineering. When I was invited to participate in this project, I considered it to be an opportunity to gain further insight on encouraging these populations to stay in engineering.

The Context of Work with Students

I mainly teach freshmen and sophomores in mechanics courses, which are fundamental-concepts courses for engineering majors. These are also required courses for all majors, including electrical and chemical, so I have many students with minimal interest in these concepts. Since I have been teaching at UW, the typical enrollment in these courses has grown from twenty-four to close to fifty students. Teaching a problems-based course to these large numbers is definitely a challenge. It is easy to lose students along the way and not notice that they are having difficulty until it is too late. Over the years, I have also noticed a change in our students, who are less inclined to be satisfied with lecture-style courses and have less success in this type of a classroom. A larger number of female students, twenty percent, and minority students, ten percent, make up our classrooms today. This compares to three percent female twenty years ago and almost no minority students. These students often have learning styles that differ from their white male counterparts.

I'm an adviser to several student organizations: the engineering honorary, Tau Beta Pi, and the senior-class honorary, Mortar Board. I'm also an adviser to the Minority Engineering Program and to the Engineering College Enrichment Fund Committee, which provides grants for student-initiated projects. Advising a student organization is a challenge. Often the officers have not developed their leadership skills, so I need to help build these skills. The students learn by doing, so it is necessary to give them the opportunity to organize and conduct events. I see my role as a support person, to provide encouragement, resources, and assistance when necessary. These experiences are among the richest that I've had in teaching. I get to truly know the students, and these relationships are sustained beyond graduation.

Teaching to the Whole Person

I find that a lot of freshmen students haven't really adjusted to the university yet. Many of them are hanging onto high school behaviors, like missing deadlines and relying on makeup work. Things going on outside the classroom are far more important to them, and they let those things interfere with their course work more than upper-level students do. You need to address these behaviors, and if you don't have an idea of what's going on in their lives, then you're fighting a losing battle.

The main thing is to try to be aware of what's going on so that when performance is lagging, there's a way to help them focus on the academic piece. The things you encounter with freshmen are varied. I recently had a student miss class and a required assignment—it wasn't a test, fortunately—for his mother's birthday. I try to get students to set their priorities and realize what they're going to have to do for the next four years.

It's difficult to know what's going on with some students—whether they're having a personal or family problem. However, many of the students share those things with you. If you're paying attention and all of a sudden a student does poorly on a test, you ask why. They may say, "Well, I was sick" or "My wife's having a baby, and she was in the hospital all night." When students do let me know they have a problem, it's in my office, after class, by email—they communicate in a variety of ways.

The Teacher-Student Relationship: Negotiating Power

It's important that there be a distinction between teacher and student; I don't try to be one of the students. I use the authority I have in the classroom to demand that students do their work and that they meet high standards. On the other hand, I want to make the students feel comfortable in asking questions during class and in coming to see me. I invite students to call me at home. I invite them to call me by my first name. I do think it's important to dress professionally, as a role model for the young women. I think power for women in the engineering classrooms is a serious issue. When I first came here, I found some faculty had difficulty making women feel comfortable and a part of the classroom.

Inside the Classroom

I try to maintain a level of authority in the classroom because, particularly when I was younger, it's easy to lose control of the classroom. If students aren't engaged, they're not learning. I think the way you approach class sets the tone. It's important that the students feel comfortable in the classroom. If they feel like the questions they ask are dumb, they're not going to ask questions. You need to show the students that you value their questions and that you're going to value them by answering their questions in a reasonable way. I have students exchange names and phone numbers because I want them to work together on their homework outside of class. These things can help open up a classroom.

I use collaborative learning methods in my classrooms. It's important that students can work together. Most engineering students have worked independently in high school and are not used to working with others. Working together effectively doesn't happen overnight—they have to be taught those skills. I try, at least twice a week, to include some collaborative work in the classroom. I monitor how the students are working together and help them develop collaborative styles. If I see students who aren't working well together, then I intervene. I also assign group work outside of class. The students know they have to work out conflicts in getting the outside project completed. I let them know that working collaboratively is an important skill required in the engineering workplace.

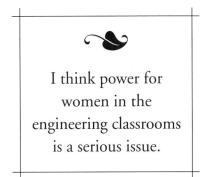

I think power for women in the engineering classrooms is a serious issue.

I use informal groups because I'm adding collaborative methods on top of a curriculum that is already full. I don't use a formal method where students are assigned roles—leader, notetaker, timekeeper, and questioner. When I interact with the groups, I talk about the various roles, and I stress that the group is responsible for every member's learning. I address shared responsibility by giving graded group quizzes. These work really well. We have ten to fifteen quizzes over the semester, approximately one a week. The students solve the quizzes as a group and agree on an answer. Performance on most of the quizzes is quite good. Participation is also good. It's interesting to note the difference between the quizzes, which are graded, and the work students do on ungraded textbook problems in class, which they tend to do individually. For the ungraded problems, I have to really encourage them to work together. When they get a quiz, however, they immediately start discussing how to solve the problem and work through it together. Sometimes students object to group work, so I try to determine the basis for their objections. I keep pushing them to work together. I give them required group assignments that they have to do together. A true conflict—students living in Cheyenne, for example—presents a major problem. A lot of students have families or work an incredible number of hours in a job, and it's difficult for them to accommodate another student's schedule. In these cases, I keep emphasizing how important it is to develop teaming skills and that they'll learn more if they work in teams. Before I make the first group assignment, I talk about why we're doing it.

Several years ago, I asked the college to spend year-end money on new furniture. Now we have tables in the classroom instead of individual desks and chairs. It's easier this way for students to collaborate and take more responsibility for their own learning. A national expert on collaborative learning, Karl Smith, the Morse-Alumni Distinguished Teaching Professor of Civil Engineering at the University of Minnesota, says that when most people first try collaborative learning, they're afraid of losing control. You do. The students are talking to each other; they're not paying any attention to you. However, if they have questions, they ask for guidance. If they're all going astray, we talk about the concept, and they go back to what they were doing.

Maintaining student attention in computer classrooms is difficult. We used a successful approach at the Colorado School of Mines, where the student computers were driven by the instructor's machine. We had a switch to turn the students' computers off, so they could see what we were doing. If I'm teaching in a computer classroom that doesn't have a switch, I'll say, "Okay, the next ten minutes I am going to demo this, and you need to take notes." After a couple of sessions, they are paying attention. But you can't lecture for very long in a computer classroom. It's not going to work when websites and email are there as distractions.

Outside the Classroom

It's important that students be involved in engineering student organizations. There, outside the classroom, they build skills that are as important in the workplace as the knowledge base they're gaining inside the classroom. I enjoy interacting with students in these organizations.

It's informal. It's not a teacher-student relationship. You learn about their families—their kids, their parents, their little sister and brother—about their aspirations, and about the things that they are interested in. You form long-term relationships—one of the best parts of teaching.

I also direct undergraduate research programs for high school and college students. I'm involved in these programs because I think it's important to get students thinking about doing research early, particularly if they're headed to graduate school. Students with experience in research labs have better chances of being accepted into the best graduate programs. I also encourage our students to seek research experiences at other universities. They meet students from across the United States and find out about programs that are available at other institutions. They can make better choices about graduate school.

Employers are looking for people who can work in teams. Interviewers are going to ask specific questions about working with other people. Companies are conducting behavioral interviews with prospective employees. They ask students, "In this situation what would you have done?" or "Describe a particularly difficult problem that you've encountered. How did you deal with it?" If graduates haven't had experience dealing with other students, they don't have anything to say. But if they've been involved in an organization or they've been in charge of a major project, they can answer these questions.

When I spent a semester teaching at the Air Force Academy, I was impressed with the emphasis on teaching and the quality of instruction that the cadets are getting. Students were expected to ask for extra instruction, or "EI," when they were having trouble; it was expected that instructors were to accommodate the students in making appointments for EI. From those sessions, I realized that there are students who benefit from additional help. So I now offer weekly group sessions. I make it clear that I don't want the A students to attend these extra sessions. The students who are having trouble need to be in an environment where they're comfortable enough to ask their "dumb" questions. After the first test, I ask all of the students who are below passing to come see me. We talk about what went wrong in the test. In some cases, I know that they'll do better on the next test, that they just made simple mistakes. In other cases, I encourage the students to attend the weekly sessions. I schedule the sessions late in the day to avoid conflicts with labs and other courses.

I also hire students to conduct several help sessions during the week for the beginning mechanics courses. I train them, to some extent, in collaborative-learning techniques—these sessions aren't simply help with homework. Since the student helpers work with students from a course with three to four different instructors, most likely the students are not working on the same homework problems. I encourage the student helpers to get the students from the same classes together so they can work on the problems together. Instructors solve problems in different ways; student helpers approach problems differently. The more ways students can look at the same problem, the better off they are.

It's interesting to note which students decide to take advantage of the sessions and which students decide not to. Some of them use the help sessions for homework. Pretty soon they show up just because that's when they're going to do their homework, and they've got a group they can do it with. Others come in because they're struggling. Some come in sporadically because they need help here and there. The same students don't consistently attend the additional sessions.

That said, in my help sessions, I refuse to do students' homework. They know that we're going to do additional problems, and they know I'll put them on the spot; they're going to have to work the problems themselves. It's an opportunity for them to clarify concepts and to ask questions about the problem-solving processes. Usually we have between five and ten students. Some of them will often say, "Could you also look at this other topic?" They get to see how other students attack problems, which is important.

Fostering All Voices

About twenty percent of the students in our engineering classrooms are women. Less than ten percent are minorities. I know from being a student in that environment, when I was the only female student in the classroom, that it's very difficult to speak up. You stand out when you ask a question and worry about asking stupid questions. You feel like you're the only person who doesn't understand the material. I finally figured out that the questions I was asking were questions others had too, so it was okay. Many of the students in this situation—the minority students, the nontraditional students—feel the same way. Nontraditional students see a bunch of eighteen-year-olds who have just taken calculus. In their mind, they don't have the mathematics background for engineering classes. It's important to make all students feel comfortable. I try to give these students opportunities outside the classroom to grapple with course concepts. I try to encourage them inside the classroom, too. When I was in school, I saw students who were treated disrespectfully. Pretty soon, these students withdrew from the class—not physically but mentally. I try to make sure that *all* of the students feel they're part of the class and that their questions are just as important as the next student's questions.

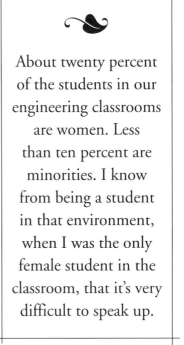

About twenty percent of the students in our engineering classrooms are women. Less than ten percent are minorities. I know from being a student in that environment, when I was the only female student in the classroom, that it's very difficult to speak up.

Gender equality can be an issue in courses where women are under-represented. There was a big push in the late 1970s and early 1980s to get more females in technical areas, and female enrollments in engineering steadily grew to about eighteen percent. Then the federal money went away, and enrollments dropped to about ten percent. The funding is back, along with emphasis on increasing minority enrollments. UW is right at the national average for female enrollments, which is twenty percent. But because of that slip to ten percent in the late 1980s, female faculty are few and far between—fewer than one percent in tenure-track ranks. Not to mention deans. There are only thirteen female deans across more than 340 institutions.

Another challenge for women in engineering is in the area of visualization. When I went through engineering school, we had two courses in graphics. During this two-course sequence, students learned to visualize in 3-D. Now, students don't take these courses. Boys use Lincoln Logs, Erector Sets, and K'Nex to build things and gain visualization skills. Women in general have less facility in visualization than their male counterparts. Young women coming into the classroom have difficulty seeing what the drawings represent, particularly for 3-D problems. Visualization skills are necessary in the mechanics courses. In the extra sessions, we work on visualization. But we're losing some of our good students because we're not helping them with these skills in the classroom.

American corporations have realized they haven't capitalized on a valuable resource and are actively recruiting women and minorities for technical fields. In engineering design teams, diversity brings a lot to the table. People solve problems differently. There are wonderful opportunities for underrepresented students. Engineering is not just sitting at a desk solving problems. There are engineering jobs that suit the nurturing tendencies of a female or that accommodate various qualities that students have, such as interacting with people.

I call on everybody in the classroom. I don't use a random technique, but I go around the classroom systematically, and I pick up where we left off the last class. This helps me see which students are struggling, and I can suggest they seek additional help. However, this technique is hindered by increasingly larger classes. In a class of twenty-four students, you can ask everybody a question every two days. When you've got forty students, it takes four days to get around the classroom. The best class I ever had was twelve students. Every student in that class mastered the content, and they all earned As and Bs. They weren't necessarily A or B students, but they had individual attention. They had a chance to ask a question whenever they needed clarification. Their tests were a pleasure to grade. With larger classes, it's getting harder to reach all the students. I have some students who drop the class when they take the first test and don't do well; they never come and talk to me, and they're gone.

Because women, men, and underrepresented populations learn differently, it's important to address these different styles in the classroom. I'm a visual learner, but there are students who learn by hearing. About once a year, a student will say, "It just all came together." This student is a global learner who puts ideas together in fits and starts and finally sees the larger picture. A student will go along earning Cs and then all of a sudden at the end of the semester, the material all makes sense. I try to allow for different learning styles in my grading scheme. If students get an A on the final, if they show they know how to do all of the work, that they understand the material, then they deserve an A for the course.

With collaborative learning, which addresses active learners, I'm seeing more success with students understanding the material. Often, students see statics as a chunk of material to master and then they're done with it. Hopefully, collaborative learning is helping them in taking these fundamental concepts on to the next courses. More than some other fields, engineering builds on previous material. Collaborative learning encourages the retention of concepts—so that students won't just memorize things for the next test.

Many students are in engineering because they want to build things, but, unfortunately, students don't get to do this in our freshman-sophomore core courses. I try to offer various activities that appeal to the different learning styles of the students. You have to recognize that you have individuals with different goals and different needs. Some are happy doing only analysis; others need to be working with their hands; and others need to look ahead at the bigger picture. In one of my classes I have developed a project that addresses these different learning styles. First, students apply mathematical analysis to trusses. Next, I provide them with a computer tool, based on the same mathematical analyses, that allows them to analyze several designs quickly. I have them build a scaled model of a truss, and then we test their model. With this assignment, students experience various modes of learning.

I was introduced to the truss assignment at the Air Force Academy, which used a military exercise as the context for the assignment. The first semester I used the truss project here, I was teaching the course with another female faculty member. My colleague changed the military exercise to an example using Doctors Without Borders, recognizing that not everyone wants to build the next rocket. This was an excellent way to reach a broader student audience.

Role Models

My instructors were all males. If I'd had a female instructor, she probably would have become a role model to me. I still don't have a role model. I started doing things I felt were important in the classroom from a hodgepodge of methods used by many of my instructors, not just a single role model.

The closest person to a role model is a math professor I had as an undergraduate. We ended up taking a teaching seminar together several years ago where we completed the Myers-Briggs Personality Test. We're identical types—not just in the same categories but at the same places on the scales. I realized why that class was the easiest class I had in college; he was teaching to me in all my preferred learning styles.

Epilogue

The university environment is wonderful for teaching because you have students who want to learn. That makes a big difference. Even when you teach required courses and not everyone is really tuned in and excited—at least they're there because they want to be. It is rewarding to see the light in a student's eyes when they master a difficult concept.

The Scholarship of Teaching and Learning: A Note on Methodology

Audrey Kleinsasser

The Warming Up the Chill project illustrates scholarship of teaching and learning methods. The scholarship of teaching and learning is an approach to understanding teaching and learning that is gaining depth and momentum in higher education. The initiative invites investigation into ways by which individual teachers or groups of teachers in a discipline frame teaching and learning. To gain deeper understanding, faculty closely examine teaching and learning through interviews, videotaped observations, reading, and in-depth case studies like the six featured in this book. One scholarship of teaching and learning goal is to better understand how students learn the elements of a discipline. Just as important, the scholarship of teaching and learning illuminates key junctures in a discipline that trip up some students.

Scholarship of teaching and learning inquiry methods include both qualitative and quantitative components, but the most important factor is making teaching public. Lee Shulman, current president of the Carnegie Foundation for the Advancement of Teaching, compares teaching to dry ice, which evaporates without a trace when exposed to oxygen. To prevent a similar evaporation of teaching, the scholarship of teaching and learning initiative aims to investigate, document, and disseminate knowledge about teaching and learning. These goals go far beyond efforts to emphasize effective approaches or to improve teaching.

At the University of Wyoming, the scholarship of teaching and learning is formally supported through the inVISBLEcollege program in the Ellbogen Center for Teaching and Learning. About to begin its fourth year, the program invites cohorts of administrators, faculty, lecturers, and graduate student teaching assistants to make a one-year commitment. During that year, the members of the cohort meet to discuss books and articles and develop classroom-based inquiry projects supported by stipends. The projects are presented at the Ellbogen Center's campus-wide colloquium in May. Some of the projects have been published or presented at national disciplinary meetings. The first inVISIBLEcollege cohort in 2000 developed a definition that guides the program's scholarship of teaching and learning efforts:

Scholarship implies peer critique, reflection, and dissemination. The scholarship of teaching enhances student learning through ongoing, systematic inquiry.

The Warming Up the Chill project, which includes a book, CD, and website, is a substantial part of the scholarship of teaching and learning initiative at UW.

Student Nominations and Formal Recognition: Phase 1

The project began in fall 2001 with student nominations. We were interested in learning from students the names of classroom teachers who value diversity as defined by age, disability, ethnicity, gender, national origin, religion, sexual orientation, or socioeconomic background. On the nomination form, we asked students to describe the organization of the class, the kinds of discussion the teacher held, office visits, assignments in the class, lectures, or readings. We asked for details about ways the teacher is skillful in teaching students from a variety of backgrounds and with different ways of knowing and learning.

We advertised the nomination process through conventional print and electronic channels with advertisements in the student newspaper and announcements on the student listserv; we also met with numerous student groups. Audrey and Jane arranged to attend and talk about the project at regular meetings of the Movimiento Estudiantil Chicano de

Aztlan (MEChA), the Minority Engineering Program/Society of Professional Hispanic Engineers, the Association of Black Student Leaders (ABSL), the Asian American Pacific Islander Student Association, the Keepers of the Fire (KOF), the Lesbian, Gay, Bisexual, and Transgender Alliance (LGBTA), the Women's Center, International Student Life, the United Multicultural Council, and the Associated Students of the University of Wyoming (ASUW). We also contacted academic support offices to meet with formally recognized student groups in each of the seven UW colleges. We invited nominations from students enrolled in distance learning courses through the Outreach School, such as interactive compressed video, audio-conference, and online courses. If we couldn't attend a meeting of the group, we emailed or telephoned the faculty or staff sponsor so students would be alerted.

Altogether, we received fifty-two nominations, some of them carefully detailed and formal and others short email transmissions. Approximately 13 percent of the nominators sought anonymity. The seven anonymous nominations reminded us that our campus is chilly in ways most teaching personnel do not anticipate. In one such letter, a UW student self-identified as transgendered wrote that the teacher clarified in an email to the student that "he had no experience with my situation. But he was willing to help me in any way he could." The student explained that on a university-sponsored trip away from Laramie, the teacher made special accommodations for the student to share a room with trustworthy friends. The teacher "has been more than willing to cultivate an environment of acceptance for me."

A public reception in December 2001 honored the fifty-two nominees and their deans and department heads. It also served to introduce the second phase of the project. Each nominee received a congratulatory letter from us that included an application to participate in the case-study phase of the project. This form, along with all of the other documents from the project, can be found on the CD-ROM that accompanies this book.

Developing the Case-Study Profiles: Phase 2

Eleven nominees completed applications for the case-study phase of Warming Up the Chill. By applying, they agreed to participate in a series of individual and small-group interviews. They also agreed to participate in public events sponsored by the Ellbogen Center. A selection panel including a member of the Ellbogen Center's Advisory Council and a student worked with Jane and Audrey to select the case-study participants. The panel considered gender, academic discipline, and academic rank. Although the final group of six represents a variety of disciplines and university services, a range of ages, and an equal representation by gender, the six were selected primarily because the set of application materials, including the student nomination, convinced the panel that each had a valuable perspective to share, wanted to learn more about himself or herself, and was committed to better serving a diverse student population.

Once selection was completed, the group of six met with Jane, Audrey, and Laurie to discuss the methodology of the case studies: videotaped interview sessions with Laurie that would then be converted into written narratives. At this point, each of the six participants signed an informed consent explaining risks and benefits of the project. Then, in a second meeting guided by Laurie, the six case-study participants selected the themes and questions that would guide the interviews. Laurie conducted individual interviews with the six participants through spring semester 2002. During this period, Laurie collected examples of syllabi, course materials, and other artifacts important to the participant's teaching. You will find these materials on the CD-ROM.

The common set of issues identified by the six participants provided the organizing structure for the narratives that Laurie constructed from the interviews. When the drafts of the cases were completed, each participant corrected factual errors, suggested deletions, and provided additions. This process is called a member check and goes beyond surface-level corrections to a deeper analysis of the interview data. During the interviewing and writing process, the nine of us participated in several public events describing the project. Questions from the audience and continued conversation prompted by the cases enabled a deepening of our theory development, included in the book's introduction. Jane edited final copies and met with each author for one final discussion.

Funding

This work was funded, in part, by grants from the University of Wyoming President's Advisory Council on Minorities' and Women's Affairs (PACMWA), the American Association of Higher Education (AAHE), and the Northern Rockies Consortium for Higher Education (NORCHE). These internal and external grants enabled us to honor the 52 nominees at a public event and with announcements in the campus and three Wyoming daily newspapers. The funding enabled us to conduct the research, publish this book, and create the CD-ROM and website that accompanies it.

Recommended Reading

To learn more about the origins of the scholarship of teaching and learning, see Ernest Boyer's *Scholarship Reconsidered: Priorities of the Professoriate*, published by the Carnegie Foundation for the Advancement of Teaching in 1990. Two books edited by Pat Hutchings, vice president at the Carnegie Foundation, provide examples of inquiry projects and consider issues raised by the initiative: *Opening Lines: Approaches to the Scholarship of Teaching and Learning* (2000) and *Ethics of Inquiry: Issues in the Scholarship of Teaching and Learning* (2002). The American Association for Higher Education has recently published *Disciplinary Styles in the Scholarship of Teaching and Learning: Exploring Common Ground* (2002), edited by Mary Taylor Huber and Sherwyn P. Morreale. Two useful websites include the Carnegie Academy for the Scholarship of Teaching and Learning (CASTL), http://www.carnegiefoundation.org/CASTL, and the American Association for Higher Education, http://www.aahe.org. The Warming Up the Chill project website is available at the Ellbogen Center's web pages, http://www.uwyo.edu/ctl.

About the Editors

Laurie Milford is a writer, editor, and faculty-development consultant living in Laramie, Wyoming. She has ten years of editing experience, working with such scholarly presses as Westview, Lynne Rienner Publishers, Basic Books, and the American Association for Higher Education (AAHE). Clients for whom she has written include the Carnegie Foundation for the Advancement of Teaching and the University of Wyoming Ellbogen Center for Teaching and Learning. Previously, Laurie directed a faculty development project at UW funded by the Hewlett Foundation. She also worked for the Carnegie Foundation to coordinate the Carnegie Academy for the Scholarship of Teaching and Learning, especially its work with the scholarly and professional societies.

Jane Nelson has directed the Writing Center at the University of Wyoming since 1991. She has worked with faculty in a variety of disciplines on classroom research projects dealing with student writing, and she has co-authored numerous articles on such subjects as computers and writing, writing center theory and practice, and writing in specific disciplines. With Kathy Evertz, Jane co-edited *The Politics of Writing Centers*, published by Boynton/Cook in 2001. She also co-edited with James Wangberg *The Ellbogen Experience: Essays on Teaching by Award-Winning University of Wyoming Faculty*, published in 2000 by the Ellbogen Center for Teaching and Learning. She received a PhD in English from the University of Utah and taught at Texas A&M University before joining the University of Wyoming in 1984.

Audrey Kleinsasser has directed the Ellbogen Center for Teaching and Learning since August 1999. As director, Audrey established UW's participation in the international scholarship of teaching and learning (SoTL) initiative through inVISIBLEcollege, a faculty development program that promotes inquiry. *Warming Up the Chill*, together with the project website, is an example of SoTL at an institutional level and UW's first such product. Also a professor in the College of Education, Audrey teaches courses in qualitative research methods. Her current scholarship focuses on ethical dilemmas in the scholarship of teaching and learning in collaboration with Mary Burman, associate dean of the College of Health Sciences at the University of Wyoming. She recently published "Researchers, Reflexivity, and Good Data: Writing to Unlearn" in *Theory into Practice* and "University Citizenship" in *About Campus*. She joined the UW faculty in 1988 after receiving a PhD in educational psychology and research from the University of Kansas.